EXTRA SUCCESS POTENTIAL

EXTRA SUCCESS POTENTIAL

*The Art of Out-Thinking and
Out-Sensing Others in
Business and Everyday Life*

Harold Sherman
and Al Pollard

PRENTICE-HALL, INC., Englewood Cliffs, N. J.

*EXTRA SUCCESS POTENTIAL The Art of Out-Thinking and
Out-Sensing Others in Business and Everyday Life*
by Harold Sherman and Al Pollard
Copyright © 1981 by Harold Sherman and Al Pollard
Address inquiries to Prentice-Hall, Inc., Englewood
Cliffs, N.J. 07632
Printed in the United States of America
Prentice-Hall International, Inc., London
Prentice-Hall of Australia, Pty. Ltd., Sydney
Prentice-Hall of Canada, Ltd., Toronto
Prentice-Hall of India Private Ltd., New Delhi
Prentice-Hall of Japan, Inc., Tokyo
Prentice-Hall of Southeast Asia Pt. Ltd., Singapore
Whitehall Books Limited, Wellington, New Zealand

10 9 8 7 6 5 4 3 2 1

Library of Congress Cataloging in Publication Data
Sherman, Harold Morrow, date
  Extra success potential.
    1. Success. 2. Interpersonal communication.
3. Extrasensory perception. I. Pollard, Al, date—
joint author. II. Title.
HF5386.S4278   650.1   80-25693
ISBN 0-13-298117-3
ISBN 0-13-298109-2 (pbk.)

This Book Is Dedicated to Your ESP-Manship

ESP is rapidly becoming recognized as the most advanced form of communication in the world today.

Within a few years, the man or woman who has not learned how to develop and use his or her higher mental faculties in communication and association with others will lose out in the race for personal growth and advancement.

Both in private life and in business, the way of thinking is radically changing. Today's world demands more dynamic mind-control methods to meet and solve personal problems—and to succeed in any business or profession.

This is leading inexorably to the realization that there is only one way left to go—and that is within the mind and heart of the individual. To the degree that you can establish a sincere empathy with another person, and be able to sense how that person really thinks and feels—just to that degree do you advance your greater success potential.

What you are actually doing, perhaps without realizing it, is calling upon your extrasensory faculties.

In so doing, you are in the process of opening up an entirely new dimension in awareness.

This new dimension is what this book is all about. It deals authoritatively with the "how to" approach in the exercise of the feeling faculties of mind in providing the specific knowledge you need to launch yourself upon the path of successful ESP-manship.

—Harold Sherman and Al Pollard

Contents

Chapter One:
The Businessman and ESP　　　　　　　　*1*
*"The individual who uses extrasensory perception
possesses an extra communication advantage."*
(Al Pollard)

Chapter Two:
**How Feelings Generate the Power
Behind Thought**　　　　　　　　　　　　*15*
*"All life basically communicates through feeling,
which is the power behind thought."*
(Harold Sherman)

Chapter Three:
**How to Transmit and Receive
Thought Images**　　　　　　　　　　　　*27*
*"Telepathy—mind-to-mind communication—is now
a recognized scientific fact." (Harold Sherman)*

Chapter Four:
**How to Recognize and Mentally Handle
Different Types of Prospects**　　　　　　*43*
*"Every individual can be reached and influenced by
a different approach, according to his type of
personality." (Harold Sherman)*

Chapter Five:
How to Size Up a Person at First Glance by ESP   57
"Your total impression of a new acquaintance is the sum total of your five senses plus your sixth sense, relating to the level of feeling." (Al Pollard)

Chapter Six:
How to Tell in Advance What a Person Is Going to Say or Do   69
"Reading the mind is really sensing the transmitted feelings of others and putting them into words." (Harold Sherman)

Chapter Seven:
How to Attune Yourself to an Individual's Personal Needs and Wants   77
"By becoming acutely aware of another person's feelings, you can sense psychological needs and material wants." (Al Pollard)

Chapter Eight:
How to Maintain Your Mental and Emotional Control So as Not to Short-Circuit Your ESP Powers   81
"Uncontrolled emotions can prevent the dependable functioning of your extrasensory power." (Harold Sherman)

Chapter Nine:
How to Know When to Sell—and When Not to Sell   89
"When you have thoroughly appealed to the wants and needs of a prospect and have built up enthusiasm, that's the time to be quiet and let the buying desire take over." (Al Pollard)

Chapter Ten:
**How to Get Accurate Impressions
of a Person Over the Telephone**   *103*
*"You can develop an ability for telephonic
telepathy." (Harold Sherman)*

Chapter Eleven:
**How to Conduct a "Mental Interview"
With a Person Before the Actual Meeting** *117*
*"Living ahead of the 'time frame' permits you to
experience others' reactions to your organized
presentation of positive picture images."
(Al Pollard)*

Chapter Twelve:
**How to Control the Thinking of a Group
Through ESP**   *127*
*"Anticipating the common denominator of feeling in
a group is the first step toward tuning in the
actions and reactions reflecting individual needs
and wants to be nourished." (Al Pollard)*

Chapter Thirteen:
**How to Change Negative Attitudes
Through ESP Sensing**   *147*
*"Negative attitudes can be neutralized with positive
mental images that create a new sense of direction
and enthusiasm leading to productive action."
(Al Pollard)*

Chapter Fourteen:
**How to Get Answers to Business and
Personal Problems in Dreams**   *157*
*"Your subconscious can be instructed to solve
problems for you in your sleep." (Harold Sherman)*

Chapter Fifteen:
How to Use ESP in Making Business
Decisions *169*
*"Sophisticated corporate leaders are turning more
and more to intuitive decisions when all the facts
are in and the final 'yes' or 'no' has to be given to
the Board of Directors." (Al Pollard)*

Chapter Sixteen:
How Women Use Their Intuition More
Than Men *183*
*"In order to achieve her goals, a woman is quicker
to tune in the feelings of others and what they
will do." (Al Pollard)*

Epilogue:
How to Use ESP in Your Everyday Life *191*
*"There is no limit to the state of awareness you can
acquire to give you daily guidance and
protection." (Harold Sherman)*

EXTRA SUCCESS POTENTIAL

Chapter One:
The Businessman
and ESP

*"The individual who uses
extrasensory perception possesses
an extra communication advantage."*
Al Pollard

To most businessmen, extrasensory perception—ESP—isn't real. They feel that even to talk about the subject, much less consider it as a new dimension for management, violates basic logic.

The simple truth is that our sixth sense is operating through us constantly. We just don't perceive it for what it is. Probably the best-known dimension of our higher powers of mind is the intuitive factor.

Most businessmen will agree they have played a strong "hunch" some time or another. And it worked. And when you get them to give the subject further consideration, they will admit that phrases like the following are not strange to them:

"I think I had better sleep on this..."

"My snap judgment is best..."

"I had a feeling you'd call me..."

"I had a mental picture of you working on that..."

"I had a premonition this was going to happen..."

"I feel like I've been through this before..."

"I had a strong urge to call you..."

"You took the words right out of my mouth..."

Mind-to-mind communication—communication without words or signs—has been proved to exist. This type of communication is not hypothetical. It is reality and is accepted by men of science who have taken the trouble to research the findings.

As more and more attention is given to the use of ESP, leading businessmen are speaking out, admitting that they have used this higher power of mind in many ways. Bill Keeler, retired chief executive officer of Phillips Petroleum Company, stated his strong feelings about the power of intuitive decisions: "After you have made your own intuitive evaluation—move boldly forward!"

Need for a New Dimension in Evaluation

There's something about using intuition in making decisions that clears away thought debris. A strong gut feeling is usually the sign that the dimension of facts has merged with the higher intellect of mind. This creative subconscious process of synthesis has focused on an answer.

Harnessing this higher intellect of mind is intriguing executives today. Some are trying to use it in a willy-nilly sort of way. Others have a tongue-in-cheek approach. Those who give this skill high priority are the ones who achieve a new dimension in management, especially in dealing with people.

The simple fact is that today's changing "people needs" and "people wants" are forcing this higher priority of mental concern. The working force of America today is smarter, more perceptive, and more demanding. Work must become more fulfilling.

Enlightened managers today are aware that an employee's psychological needs are just as real as his or her material wants. In fact, we hear more about employee morale in addition to money paid for productive services.

Dr. Rinsis Likert, University of Michigan, conducted a milestone piece of research pointing up this need for "psychic pay." In his approach to this subject, he interviewed thousands of white- and blue-collar workers and hundreds of top managers.

He asked managers to list in order of priority, one through 10, their perception of things most important to their employees on the job. Then he asked employees to list one through 10 the things they considered most important to their job.

As you might suspect, the two lists were inverted.

Management listed at the top "material gains," whereas employees listed as number one, "appreciation for work done." And number two: "being in on things." They placed material gains toward the bottom of their list!

In other words, the managers who have a sixth sense feeling for their employees' psychic needs are decades ahead of those managers who manage "by the numbers" and through fear. The cost of training employees today makes it important "by the numbers" to reduce turnover. People do not leave jobs when they feel they are appreciated and are important enough to be "in on things."

In trying to understand these new employee demands, top management is painfully aware of the need for new dimensions in evaluating what can be done in the name of "good business." Few corporate leaders in America today are truly sensitive to the feelings of their fellow executives—much less to the feelings of workers on the line.

Yet there is no compromise with the fact that goals and objectives must be met on schedule. The constant pressure to make a corporate profit for dividends large enough to attract public money for expanded production calls for more and more effective ways of gaining greater productivity through people.

It is a known fact that a person interested in his or her work will be inspired to perform at optimum ability. Much has been done and said in the name of motivation. Yet "motivation" is a hollow word that fails to convey the depth of an internal desire to perform at peak ability.

For executives, supervisors, and line workers, achieving that basic type of internal inspiration is a new and exciting challenge. It must be met with a greater understanding of people—and of what makes them tick.

This is where the higher powers of mind can be of greatest service. Becoming deeply aware of personal feelings is the beginning of intuitive management.

Whether you call these higher powers extrasensory perception, precognition, or intuition is of little consequence. It's the end result that counts.

Mind Energy—the Unknown Force

Scientists cannot explain or quantify the power of mind energy. They have no instruments to measure the amazing examples of the mind force at work.

I am recalling an experience by our good friend Ingo Swann, a fine artist in New York. Also a biologist, Ingo has great respect for the precision of scientific investigation. He is a psychic, too, and when he started giving serious consideration to his unusual mental gifts, he began to think he was mentally unbalanced. In fact, he wasn't quite sure what he was.

He could not distinguish between imagination and psychic impressions in his mind, so he made a logical move. In the early seventies, he contacted the Stanford Research Institute and stated he would like to involve himself with their scientists in controlled tests of his unusual perceptions. Ingo has been given more tests by Stanford Research Institute than any other psychic. Their investigators are still shaking their scientific heads over the amazing things Ingo can perform whenever he desires.

Ingo tells his first experiences with SRI in his intriguing book, *To Kiss Earth Goodbye.*

The first experience completely baffled the top physicists who monitored his experiment. He was asked to stand in the middle of a bare room and look down at the concrete floor to see if he could concentrate on moving the needle of a magnetometer below.

Ingo, a delightful person with a wry sense of humor, was rather amused and surprised at being asked to concentrate through a concrete floor. But he did.

After about five minutes, he released his intense concentration on moving the needle. He looked at the scientists in charge and asked if the needle had moved. "Yes, it moved" was the answer, marked with quiet incredulity.

The truly amazed scientists couldn't believe what they had observed. They told Ingo that he was standing in a room in which the United States government had invested millions of dollars to create an environment that could screen out all energy waves. They pointed out that the concrete floor was three feet thick and that the magnetometer was protected by five feet of lead. His mind energy had apparently penetrated the energy shields.

As you might expect, they asked Ingo to try again. Results were the same: the needle moved. But after being asked to repeat this experiment several times, Ingo became somewhat exasperated.

"Look," he said, "get me a piece of paper and a pencil." He began to draw quickly. In a few moments he finished his sketch and held it out to the observing scientists. "Is this an accurate sketch of the installation you have under all this concrete and lead?"

Again the quiet answer was "Yes."

Thus Ingo Swann, artist and biologist, discovered he wasn't crazy, nor was he imagining things. He now knew that his ability to send his mind to remote environments was a proven fact.

Although he was delighted to make this discovery,

the physicists were thoroughly confounded in their attempts to measure or quantify this unusual power of
mind energy.

Today, thousands of tests later with Ingo, the
scientists are still unable to get a handle on mind energy.
Just as Dr. J. B. Rhine proved that intelligence can be
transferred from mind to mind, so Ingo Swann has proved
that consciousness can be sent short and long distances in
what is called remote viewing.

We tell you this story because to us it proves beyond a shadow of a doubt that the mind of man can tune
in on universal energy in many interesting ways.

This is why we feel that when it comes to getting
unusual impressions beyond usual capabilities, every
businessman should take the time to experiment in developing his own God-given powers—which extend beyond
the accepted five senses.

Awareness—a Business Tool That Can Be Sharpened and Polished

In speaking to business leaders around the country, we
find that most feel ESP is an interesting subject but
doesn't have much to do with them personally.

At the end of each talk, however, eight or ten men
and women usually come to the front. Here are some of
the more common questions they ask:

"Do you really feel that everyone has this ESP
ability?"

"How do you go about developing this higher
power of mind?"

"Do you use ESP in running your own business?"

"Can you teach people to use their ESP abilities?"

"Do young people have more ESP ability than older people?"

"Are women more sensitive than men with ESP?"

There are many other questions, of course, and we're happy to report that more and more businessmen and businesswomen are taking this subject seriously. Because of this widening interest, we decided it was time to write a book like this one to give our best answers to these and other serious questions.

Perhaps the starting point in helping businessmen and women understand their sixth sense is to simply say that we are talking about increasing awareness.

For us, this is the key word in probing the higher powers of our God-given mind. Hence the immediate question becomes "Awareness of what?"

In answering that broad question, we must quickly admit that each of us is already aware of many things. Your daily life makes you pay attention to traffic laws, driving safety, diets, your baby's health, how much to drink, the boss's temperament, mistakes in your work, your bank account, the cost of food and gasoline, and so on.

These are the usual concerns you have as you go along day after day. It's a simple survival pattern of awareness in an industrial society. At this level, however, you are using only your five senses.

Naturally, the better you use them, the better you get along in our world of give-and-take relationships. If we go in a different direction, in another time, however, and think of the American Indian prior to the white man's arrival, we have an entirely different level of awareness for survival.

It doesn't take much imagination to understand why these earth people living close to Mother Nature were so sensitive to all of their natural environment.

Their five senses were developed far beyond any degree of the white man's today. Survival for an Indian brave meant he must find food, overcome enemies, provide shelter, and relate to the Great Spirit in the Sky.

These basic challenges taught him to use all of his senses—including his sixth sense. Every young brave was taught to see with the eye of an eagle, listen with the intensity of a hunted animal, smell with the accuracy of the grazing buffalo, feel with the sensitivity of the honeybee on a flower, and taste with the sharpness of the arrow's point.

In addition to these highly developed five senses, the early American Indian also had a highly developed sixth sense. He could sense the changing of seasons long before squirrels began burying nuts, or the fish began to spawn, or the waterfowl went winging across the sky to warmer weather.

He knew because he knew. He could read the signs of the forest and sky like a book. His instincts were sharp and accurate. He was a part of the whole, an extension of the universe and all of its glorious parts. He liked nothing better than to sit completely still and experience the earth, the sky, the Great Spirit. He was completely aware—for survival.

Awareness of People Sharpens Your Senses for Feeling

Just as the Indian became acutely aware of his physical environment to survive, so we, living as close to one another as we do today, need to become acutely aware of other people—not just to survive but to enjoy living.

What do we mean by awareness of people? For the most part, we're referring to a sense of feeling for their psychological needs and material wants. Within these two areas, most of us live our lives either in quiet desperation or with inspired purpose.

If you are to feel you are a part of the world around you, it is imperative that you use your best intuitive insight to pick up signals being given off by those around you at any given moment in time.

In a later chapter, we will be giving specific details on how to attune yourself to the specific needs and wants of others, how to share supportive ideas that will create harmony and enthusiasm. Here, for example, is the kind of awareness we mean:

My wife and I dropped in for a bite of lunch at a Dobbs House restaurant in the Memphis Airport while waiting for our airplane to arrive. After we settled down at our table and scanned the menu, an attractive young waitress caught my attention. She was darting from table to table.

I could observe customers giving her a hard time about her service. Obviously they were under stress to meet departing planes. So it became clear that both customer and waitress were under a similar mental strain.

When she finally came to get our order, I could sense she was nervous and ill at ease, but she was quietly polite. I was pleased to see how quickly she served our club sandwiches. As we enjoyed eating leisurely, I continued watching our waitress trying to please her customers—who continued to give her the rush act, along with a hard time of criticism.

Since we weren't in a hurry, we sat and enjoyed sipping our coffee while the crowd thinned out. After a few minutes, the waitress came to our table. As she handed me the check, I smiled at her and told her how much we appreciated the good service she had given us and what a fine job she was doing.

To my surprise, tears began to trickle down her face. She tried to brush them aside so they wouldn't be noticed. Feeling that I had done something wrong, I asked her if I had said something to upset her.

"You don't understand," she said. "This is my first day on the job, and yours is the first kind word I've heard. Everyone else has been screaming at me about what a sorry waitress I am. It's been terrible!"

What she said was not surprising. It was obvious she wasn't a seasoned waitress who could take customer complaints in stride. It was also clear to a concerned observer that she needed a bit of encouragement. My kind words of appreciation broke the dam of her pent-up emotion. As I gave her the money for our check, I told her that I was going to write a secret on my napkin that would turn her life around. But she wasn't to read it until we had gone.

Looking back over my shoulder as we walked out the door, I saw her reach for the napkin and read my secret. It was a short message that simply said: "You will always succeed in life if you will always think and act in terms of the other person's self-interest."

The *Feeling* Response Is Most Important

As you can see from this simple story, I was quick to pick up this young waitress's feelings simply because I tuned in to her emotional need at the moment.

Nothing I could have said to her would have been as important as those sincere words of appreciation. Her inner self was crying out for help, but she wasn't aware of her distress signal. I became aware because I cared. I took the time and energy to project myself into her aura of feelings.

In other words, I had a strong intuitive feeling that appreciation was the specific feeling that needed to be broadcast to her. As we know, the hunger for appreciation is one of the most powerful psychological needs in the world of human beings. Even animals are quick to respond to appreciation. And in a stressful situation such as this young waitress was experiencing, appreciation is doubly important.

All of which takes us back to the basic idea that awareness is the key to intuitive feelings. I had to become aware of this waitress in distress before I could tune her in and get an intuitive fix on her psychological need.

Great Organizations Reflect a People-Oriented Chief Executive Officer

As we study top executives capable of building great organizations, it becomes clear that most of them are people-oriented. They *care* about people. They are more aware of people. They know how to relate to their top managers in a way that inspires greatest effort.

In addition, detailed studies of these top executives have pointed out that they rate high in ESP capabilities. For some reason, these leaders have strong intuitive feelings about people around them and coming events. They are, in fact, making use of their God-given sixth sense. They know that the intuitive feeling is a force that can be harnessed. They have faith in this idea, and they make it work. Like all people who become proficient in any field, they practice, practice, practice. And yet I have met some top executives who have a still greater gift of intuition. They have a highly developed sense of *knowing without experiencing*. None of them can explain how they arrive at what they intuitively know.

Strange as it may seem, the rise of the computer has helped to bring more emphasis to the "gut level" decision process. As executives who work with computer printouts know, the computer is great at telling you *what*, but does not give much help in telling you *why*. Answers to "why" call for creative synthesis of factual input. So far, man's unconscious mind has no peer in this creative process.

Chapter Two: How Feelings Generate the Power Behind Thought

"All life basically communicates through feeling, which is the power behind thought."

Harold Sherman

All selling starts and ends with feeling.

What would it be worth to you to know as much about the other fellow as you can come to know about yourself? To be able to sense how he is feeling about you or a product or a service before he makes his feelings known—no matter what he is saying to you or hasn't said? Wouldn't this acquired ability add immeasurably to your selling power—and to your awareness of life in general?

This is what ESP can do for you once you learn how to develop and use it. You've been hearing a great deal about it lately. But what essentially *is* extrasensory perception?

The new science of parapsychology, which has to do with researching ESP, defines it as "the functioning of the higher powers of mind beyond the reach of the five physical senses."

These powers manifest themselves in the form of dreams, visions, apparitions, impressions of things to come (precognition); mind-to-mind communication (telepathy); the ability to mentally see and hear things at a distance (clairvoyance and clairaudience); the movement or influencing of material objects by mind (psychokinesis); out-of-body experiences (astral projection); messages from discarnate entities (mediumship); and so on.

The phase of ESP that should command your personal interest and that possesses the most practical value, however, is the ability you can develop to communicate *feelingly* with others.

It has not been generally recognized as yet, but *feeling is actually the universal language.* You have to feel before you find words to express your feelings. This is the very essence of extrasensory perception. Feeling always generates the power behind thought. It has an energy, a transmitting force. It projects itself in the form of mental images with feeling behind them.

To a degree, you are influenced by how the people with whom you are associated react to you emotionally. You may not be conscious of this influence in the way you respond to others—but it is all a result of the intensity of their feelings. They, in turn, are affected by your thoughts and feelings concerning them.

If you accept these statements, you can begin to understand that at present there is much of your mind and its great potentialities that you are not consciously and intelligently using. It is our aim to present this knowledge to you in a way that you can apply with profit and benefit in your business as well as private life.

As you proceed, never lose sight of the fact that feeling is the motivating force behind all life and that you are constantly selling yourself or being sold, through feeling, with everything you do.

Outer space is getting a lot of attention these days, but the space that should concern you most is the inner space of your own mind. This space contains the machinery of your mind—the most sensitized, fantastic instrument in the universe. Whether or not you have fully realized it before, whatever success you achieve in life depends on how you care for your mind and what use you make of it.

You probably tend to take the possession of your mind for granted. You came into the world with it, and it has been functioning for you, after a fashion, since the day you were born. You've used it as a storehouse, filling your memory with all manner of mental images of past experiences, from the time of your first baby cry to this present moment. Every incident and event, however big or small, has been recorded and always will be—filed automatically in the computerized section of your brain, ready for instant recall and replay when needed.

You've heard the old bromide likening the mind to the iceberg: Only one eighth is exposed to view above the surface, while seven eighths is submerged. You've been told that your conscious mind is limited by your five physical senses, which, in this one-eighth "above water" area, are reporting only what you can see, hear, taste, touch, and smell.

What is happening in the remaining seven eighths of your mind, beyond the awareness level of consciousness, no one pretends to know exactly.

So here you are, with all your vaunted education, experience, and training, not so smart as you may have thought you were; certainly not as smart as you *can* be if you can learn how to lift yourself more and more above the surface—and thereby expand your awareness.

What exists in this "submerged part" of yourself? Well, for one thing, your mysterious but wonderful extra-sensory perceptive faculties. You've been using them, off and on, all your life, but you have seldom been conscious of this fact. They have "surfaced" in moments of need, and given you flashes of feeling to do or not to do something, which you may have recognized and even obeyed.

Are you now willing to agree that the time has come for you to look within yourself and try to find out what is there? What thoughts and feelings you have accumulated, through the years, that constitute excess baggage? Are they actually cluttering up your mind and getting in the way of your clear thinking?

If you take a good look, you may make the painful discovery that many of the ills and unhappy happenings you have been blaming on others have been the result of your own wrong thinking. In other words, you have not been making proper use of the instrument of your mind.

Should you be employed in the business or industrial world, you are necessarily a part of a large organization. Whatever your position, you have been trained to be part of the team, each member "doing his thing," it is hoped, to the best of his ability.

To a great extent, the success of the company depends on the degree of efficiency of operation. If some individuals in important segments become disturbed, for whatever reason, and fall down on their jobs, they can throw serious monkey wrenches into the company's ordinarily smooth functioning.

The same applies to the organization of your mind. Feed it mental images of fear, worry, hate, resentment, prejudice, or other destructive thoughts, and you can greatly impair its normally helpful operation. These wrong mental images can foul up your thinking and keep you from making right decisions or judgments.

Take a look—they may have been doing it for years!

Science, up to the present moment, has been too concerned with creating weapons of destruction to invest much time or money in researching the mind. The human mind has had the capacity to invent atomic bombs as well as kitchen gadgets, but hasn't been able to understand itself. Might as well confess it—don't you know more about the working parts of your automobile than you do your own mind?

Of course, having a car is most important, and if it breaks down, you're often in real trouble. But your mind—which you have depended upon for everything that has happened to you and upon which your whole future thoughts and actions leading to success or failure depend—is still pretty much a mystery to you, permitted to function on its own. If something goes wrong with your mind's operation, resulting in a mental or nervous breakdown, you usually find yourself powerless to fix it and are driven to a doctor or psychiatrist to give you pills or couch or shock treatments. Ironically enough, you know the least about the most valuable, absolutely indispensable and irreplaceable mechanism you possess!

It's little wonder that you haven't discovered nor

learned how to make use of some of the more or less hidden powers of your mind. You've had experiences that you have usually put down to happenstance or coincidence wherein you have had an urgent "feeling" to do or not to do something, and have disregarded such feelings only to be sorry later. At one time or another, you have also probably had a fleeting vision or dream that you subsequently recognized as having been a premonition of a coming event—but you have paid little conscious attention to these occurrences or taken time to explore the why and how of your mind's occasional awareness of such things. Actually, nothing in this universe happens by accident. There is a cause behind everything, however big or small. And in the area of human life, we are setting up most of these causes by our own thinking, wrong or right.

It's not so difficult to gain an understanding of your mind and how it operates. This can be explained in a comparatively few words. But it takes longer to eliminate from your mind all the wrong ideas and concepts you have accumulated through the years which have put carbon in the cylinders and congested its working parts.

It's been clearly outlined in Harold Sherman's previous Prentice-Hall book, *The New TNT—Miraculous Power Within You,* just how your mind functions—how you think basically in mental pictures. Associated with every subconsciously stored image of everything that has happened to you is the feeling, or emotional reaction, you had at the time. Your mental attitude toward life and others today, and toward yourself, is based on your images of the past. As you have changed your thoughts and feelings about anyone and anything, your attitude has changed, of course. But strong fears, or hates or prejudices or feelings of inferiority that have been deeply rooted in consciousness, will set up disturbances in your present and future, until they're removed.

This is because of a great and unfailing law of

mind: *like always attracts like.* Put simply: Think good thoughts, they will eventually attract good things. Think bad thoughts, they will eventually bring bad things to pass.

You possess a remarkable creative power in mind which apparently functions magnetically. Give it a mental picture of something you want (or something you fear) and it starts to work, like a faithful servant having no reasoning power, using the picture as a blueprint to attract all the conditions necessary to bring about the externalization of what you have wanted—or feared.

These conscious thoughts of yours, which have given the blueprint of what you want or fear to your creative power, have set up the causes that will always lead to effects after their kind. Wrong thinking can produce wrong results as unerringly as right thinking can produce right results. The law of mind is inexorable. You as a creature of free will can use this instrument of your mind to help make or break you.

Never forget this! And remember, too, that your feelings always generate the power behind your thoughts. The more *intensely* your feelings are related to what you want or fear, the more quickly you can expect these things to happen. The more concentrated power, the more action. People with big dreams quite often have to share this blueprint, and through salesmanship arouse the feelings of many others to help make their dreams come true. But whether you work by yourself, as an individual, or with others, it is feeling that sells an idea or a product or a service. And it is the higher powers of mind that get the job done.

I can agree intellectually with everything you say in your "sales pitch," but you can never get me to buy unless you move me emotionally—unless you arouse in me the *desire* to buy.

All selling, therefore, has to be emotional in

nature! You have to have a feeling for the prospect as well as a feeling for your product—and you have to know how to communicate both—or there is no sale!

What has been sold through feeling? Let's browse around through history!

Cleopatra, for example, didn't do so badly as a saleswoman. She aroused feelings in Julius Caesar and Mark Antony for her and sold them both a bill of goods that "raised Cain" with the world in her time. However, she failed to sell Octavian, and I wish we had the intimate details of this failure so we could judge what went wrong with her sales pitch. It might throw some light on why some of our feminine TV pitch artists don't excite the buying desires of viewers.

Another woman did fairly well. She was just a girl with an idea, but having made this sale, she so aroused the feelings of the people of France that they accepted her as their leader. You know what Joan of Arc was able to do as a result.

Christopher Columbus had rough going as a salesman for many years until he finally got Ferdinand and Isabella steamed up about giving him money and ships to reach the East Indies—as he thought—by sailing west. He missed the bull's eye, but hit a much bigger target. We have profited from his salesmanship ever since.

P. T. Barnum was a super salesman who discovered early in life that he could sell the public anything by dressing it up and making it sound and look attractive. Said Barnum, "There's a sucker born every minute!" He proved it by appealing again and again to the wonder and curiosity and eternal craving for new thrills in the emotional nature of that queer little creature classified as *Homo sapiens*! People paid to be fooled—and loved it!

Henry Ford answered the crying need of a people trying to escape from the "horse and buggy" age by development and mass production of his famous Model T. He sold it to this emotionally hungry buying public at a price all could afford to pay. But he didn't stop there. He saw to it that his "tin lizzie" was constantly in the minds of the people by instructing his then-small advertising department to collect, originate, and disseminate all manner of jokes on his Ford car. Newspapers reprinted these jokes by the zillions, giving them a local flavor. And citizens everywhere, with a developed affection for the Ford car, were actually laughed into buying!

Mahatma Gandhi proved that force is not necessary in selling, but that emotional appeal *is*. His passive resistance campaign captured the sympathy and interest of the world and sold the British people on granting independence to India.

Casanova, the famous Latin lover, had little or no money, but he didn't need it. His one stock in trade was romance. He made a commodity of sex appeal, which he sold with such charm and wit that women, wherever he traveled throughout Europe, were ready, waiting, and willing to succumb to his devastating sales pitch. Even rulers, influenced by his vast personal popularity, felt it was smart to welcome him as a "conquering hero." Today, salesmen are still doing business and always will, Casanova style, on the sound emotional premise that "All the world loves a lover"! (Love that man, love his product!)

When men and women get hot and bothered about something, they are moved to do something about it! And when emotionally aroused, they can of course be moved in the wrong direction as well as the right. Think what a salesman Hitler was! The feelings he aroused in the German people—and the terrible consequences of his selling them into a world war! (Never underrate a man with an audience, when he is on fire!)

Franklin Delano Roosevelt was one of the greatest salesman this world has ever known. He talked the American people out of the Great Depression—with his fireside chats, his New Deal philosophy, and his famous statement, repeated over and over until it was dinned into mass consciousness: "We have nothing to fear but fear itself."

This masterful selling stabilized the emotions of the people, gave them new hope, cheer, self-confidence, and resolution. They bought what FDR had to offer— *four* times!

No one took Harry S Truman too seriously when he became President. They sympathized with the enormous burdens he was compelled to assume, but they soon discovered that they had sold Harry short. Harry Truman scored one of the greatest one-man-selling victories in all political history. His singlehanded crusade to re-elect himself President, his never-say-die spirit, and his terrific underdog fight so aroused the feelings of the voters that they stormed to the polls and knocked out the favorite-to-win, Thomas E. Dewey, who had thought all he had to do was to shadowbox his way into the White House!

Adlai Stevenson had the words and the ideas, but he didn't have the knack of humanizing them with sufficient *feeling* to reach and move a large enough sector of the voting public. Though Eisenhower lacked Stevenson's polish and wit and often "murdered the King's English," he proved the better salesman. People, having originally accepted him as their military leader, were conditioned to accept him in this new role. When he entered their living rooms, his informal manner made them feel closer to him, warmer, and more comfortable—easy pushovers for the personal-sounding "We like Ike" slogan, which they shouted in a mighty chorus of votes!

No candidate can ever win who does not stir the emotions of the people. When two strong candidates have equal emotional appeal, the sentiments of the people are almost evenly divided. Never forget that the masses do not think with their minds—they think with their *emotions*. What they feel, they do. What they do *not* feel, they do *not* do!

When your prospect says, "I don't feel..." you can be sure he is not in the mood to buy. You might better pack your sales kit and arrange to see him in the sweet bye and bye, because you haven't gotten through to him. And if you press beyond this point, he may raise his emotional defenses so high that you'll *never* sell him!

If you arouse a prospect's interest but not his feelings, you only soften him up for the next salesman. The moment a fellow comes along who knows how to reach him emotionally, he will capitalize upon the prospect's awakened interest.

Study the great religious leaders of the world. All were terrific salesmen. They sold ideas of regeneration and salvation that lodged in the hearts of untold millions.

Jesus, after presenting his "spiritual selling pitch," ended with the simplest closing line in all recorded history, when he said two little words: "Follow me!" Since the expression of his philosophy and the utterance of these two words, countless humans of all races in every age, down to our present day, have purchased his offer with their faith and devotion.

Note, in all instances, how great masses of people in all times and in all countries on the face of this earth have been moved by *one* individual, not through high intellectual but through great *emotional* appeal!

You can sell anything, good or bad, to a lot of people, if you get aroused enough about it. Their feelings will be moved by yours, and once they *feel* with you, they will *act* with you! Afterward, some of them may say they don't know why they did what they did; they think they may have been temporarily mesmerized by their feelings. But, nevertheless, they did what their feelings at the moment *dictated*! This, of course, was the objective of the one who sold them!

No question about it, the top salesmen of the world are dealing with a great, unlimited power—inspiring, and at the same time, frightening in its potentiality. To fully appreciate this, you have only to consider that a spellbinding orator given the mediums of radio, television, and the press can become a colossal force for good or evil—depending upon what he is selling!

So, put this in your salesman's pipe and smoke it:

You—whoever you are, whatever you are, wherever you are—can vastly increase your selling power once you learn how to put greater *emotional appeal* behind your sales pitch.

The time to start making these extrasensory faculties work for you is now!

Chapter Three:
How to Transmit and Receive Thought Images

"Telepathy—mind-to-mind communication—is now a recognized scientific fact."

Harold Sherman

Whether you realize it or not, you are surrounded by thought vibrations from the minds of others. They seldom reach your conscious awareness because you are ordinarily protected by what I call "an electromagnetic insulatory shield," which constantly tunes out what is of no interest or value to you.

You know that you can turn the dial of your radio or television set from one station to another and get any program you want, eliminating all others that are broadcasting at the same time. Your mind's mechanism operates in a similar manner. It is governed by the universal or cosmic law of "like always attracting like."

Thought impulses from the minds of others are either accepted or rejected by virtue of their law of attraction, and every experience you have had or are to have is dictated by your likes or dislikes. Whatever this creative power within you wants, it magnetizes conditions around you to help you get. What it doesn't want, it closes mental doors against. The acceptance or rejection of thoughts works the same way.

You cannot think a thought without transmitting it. Every human being everywhere is doing it all the time, every waking moment. Your feelings generate the power behind the thoughts that are projected. Feeling is actually the universal language. Your thought images, once emanated from consciousness, are kept alive in what I call "the mental ether" by the electromagnetic energy field. That's how it is possible for a sensitive-minded person to pick up images and feeling impressions of something that has happened to an individual or something he is thinking about at the moment.

Let me give you a graphic, well-documented illustration of one of my own experiences in the receiving and transmission of thought.

Ivan Tors, well-known television and film producer, tells about a telepathic test to which I was subjected. He had hired scientists at UCLA as technical advisers on a TV series he was making called *The Man and the Challenge*. The test took place in a UCLA laboratory in the presence of three medical doctors and psychologist Leslie LeCron, on the night of January 18, 1960.

At the time, Tors's show was exploring the limits of the human body and mind, and one subject Tors had selected to dramatize was ESP. He had developed an interest in me through having read the Wilkins-Sherman book *Thoughts Through Space*, covering our experiments in long-distance telepathy. He had met me personally over a luncheon at the Hollywood-Roosevelt Hotel and been impressed by my apparent sensitivity. But with all this, he had remained a disbeliever.

In the Introduction to my book *How to Make ESP Work for You*, Tors told how UCLA scientists invited me to take part as an observer in the test of a noted medium, Sophia Williams. I did not anticipate being called upon to give a demonstration of my own, but when I arrived at the laboratory, the psychiatrist in charge informed me that Sophia Williams had been taken ill and could not be present. He explained that it was not easy for these men to assemble at the same time, and since Tors had told them about my telepathic experiments with Wilkins some years before, would I mind taking Sophia Williams' place and submit to an investigation in her stead?

I asked the medical doctors what they would like me to attempt.

"We would like to have you see if you can duplicate what you did with Wilkins. Tors tells us that three nights a week from 11:30 to midnight, you sat in your study in New York, made your mind receptive, and recorded such impressions as came to you from the mind of Wilkins, who was in the Far North, searching for lost Russian fliers. He would get off by himself and concentrate his mind on you, reliving and reviewing the outstanding things that had happened to him that day."

"That is correct," I replied.

"We also understand that you made copies of whatever impressions came to you and put them in the mail that same night, addressing them to Dr. Gardner Murphy, director of the Psychology Department of Columbia University, for him to check and eventually confirm."

"That's true," I assented.

What I did not know at the time was that the scientists had expressed doubt when Tors told them of my *Thoughts Through Space* experiments. They pointed out that these tests had taken place quite some years ago, and how could they be sure of such findings today? It was suggested that if I could be brought to the laboratory and subjected to the same experiment, they did not believe I could produce similar results.

Now, however, the circumstances had been brought about, and I was being propositioned to undertake just such a test.

"We would like to determine if you can do with Tors what you did with Wilkins. He has been on location all day shooting a sequence for his television show. We would like you to remain in this office while we take Tors down the corridor to a remote room and have Leslie LeCron place him under light hypnosis. Let Tors relate to us what has happened to him and his camera crew and actors today. While we are doing this, we'd like you to take the next half hour to record, from Tors's mind, what impressions may come to you. Is this all right?"

"It's all right with me," I said. "However, it won't

be necessary for you to hypnotize Tors. Whatever has happened to him today is already recorded in his subconscious mind . . . and if I am successful in tuning in, I'll get the images from his subconscious."

"Well, we think we'll hypnotize him just the same," said the medical doctor.

In the case of the UCLA experiment, one might say the scientists had me just where they wanted me. Had they arranged for such a test in advance, and had I been as successful, they could have charged that I must have obtained a knowledge of what had happened to Ivan Tors that day, by some physical means.

Calling upon me to submit to a test on the spur of the moment, however, obviously gave me no time to prepare—were I, or any sensitive, disposed so to do. Ivan Tors, in his statement, has made this point clear. I am sure that the medical doctors, believing that mind-to-mind communication was impossible, were certain that I could not produce any evidential results.

I am giving you now the first published account of how I felt during the half hour of this challenging test.

I now admit to a flashing feeling that I was being tricked into the test, wondering if the scientists had used a medium as an excuse for getting me there as an observer, so they could create ideal conditions for "putting me on the spot." However, I put these thoughts aside and readily agreed to the proposal.

I was given pencils and sheets of paper, seated at a desk in the doctor's office, and the group went out and locked the door. Apparently they were taking no chances of my possibly getting out, slipping down the hall, and putting my ear to the keyhole where they were—and then rushing back and recording what I heard!

Many scientists' and magicians' first thoughts are of the possibility of trickery—and there is some justification for this since there are, unhappily, many fraudulent practices.

Tors now takes up the account:

"Harold Sherman was placed in a small office with the doors closed. He remained there for thirty minutes to jot down his impressions, if any.

"We left Sherman behind locked doors and our group proceeded to its location. We closed the door and Leslie LeCron placed me under a light degree of hypnosis."

As I prepared my mind to attempt to tune in on Tors's subconscious, I ran up against a wall of skepticism emanating from the minds of the medical doctors.

You must remember, we are all broadcasting our thoughts, impelled by the feelings we have at the time. But the average person is not aware of the thoughts of others unless they come in on his "wavelength." By this I mean that like thoughts and like feelings attract like thoughts and feelings—as when a husband and wife, for example, express the same words or ideas at the same time.

When I made my mind receptive and sought contact with Tors's mind, my first encounter was a wave of feeling from the medical doctors whose minds were on me, and who were watching Leslie LeCron in the act of placing Tors under hypnosis.

When you run into such a resistant force, it is a blocking sort of sensation. It is like running into static when trying to bring in a radio program on a specific station. I knew I would have to demagnetize myself from these negative feelings, or my mind could not be a clear channel for getting the thought images I would be seeking from Tors's subconscious.

I instantly resorted to the technique I had used, years before, in reaching the mind of Wilkins some two or three thousand miles away, when he was preparing to send me thought images on what had happened to him in the Far North.

The technique is a form of concentrated suggestion. I instructed my mind to "Determine for me what has happened this day to Ivan Tors while shooting a picture wherever he may be."

As I directed my conscious mind's attention to the mind of Tors, I bypassed the thought waves—if I may call them that—emanating from the minds of the medical doctors. I felt their waves of skepticism fall away from me, and I began to see images in my mind's eye, and to receive strong feelings from Tors's consciousness.

Take note that my suggestion pertained to "this day" only! Otherwise, I would have found myself in the memory stream of the subconscious, having to do with recorded experiences dating back to the time of Tors's birth. Not that I couldn't range back and forth among these myriad images, but a sensitive might well pick up impressions of some of the most deeply felt experiences of a lifetime unless his attention was centered upon a certain specific time period.

Using this technique with Wilkins, I found I was able to limit my awareness just to the days when we had set up for mind-to-mind communication. And now I was glad to see that a flow of images was coming to me in response to this same method, as I began recording my first impression.

"In this light trance," Tors recounts, "I was asked to relate everything I had done that day.

"It was a very unusual day—the start of a new film, and I had spent most of the day at sea. We dropped divers from a helicopter into the ocean and picked them up. We strafed a stunt man with machine-gun bullets. A new portable air-to-sea communication system was used for the first time. During the filming of this sequence, the machine gun jammed, and I had to change the shooting schedule, which made me quite upset.

"The next sequence photographed was on a diving boat equipped with a torpedolike object, a portable decompression chamber. At this time I had to take over the direction of the scene as I was the only one present who actually had seen a decompression chamber in operation under emergency conditions, treating a man who had the bends, and I had to instruct our very able director how to do it correctly.

"In the meantime, I ordered one of the seamen to throw a weighted line overboard with a marker to show our position for another scene. In the next sequence, we had to throw a small explosive charge overboard to signal to the divers with sound repercussions.

"While I was talking about these very complicated and technical scenes of which nobody there but myself could have had any knowledge, one of the doctors purposely inflicted pain upon me. He wanted to see whether Sherman would pick up the pain reaction. At another time they stabbed the back of my hand with a needle and squeezed my right ear."

The impressions kept on coming, not in the order of their actual happenings during the day, but usually determined by the intensity of feelings that Tors had experienced in reacting to the events.

The other scenes rapidly followed, looking in consciousness much as you might recall scenes from memory of a motion picture you may have seen.

I seemed to be a spectator of these happenings. Quite often I couldn't catch them all, but could get enough of them so that they were recognizable, and often so specific that the whole happening came through.

I got the feeling at the very moment that Leslie LeCron was bringing Tors out from under his light hypnotic trance, and recorded the time. I was sitting, relaxed, waiting for the return of the group when the half hour was up.

After unlocking the door, the leading doctor entered, followed by the others: "Well," he asked me in a skeptical tone of voice, "did you get anything?"

For answer, I handed him the four pages of notes. He looked at them in amazement.

"Read them," he said.

"No, you read them," I requested.

"Thirty minutes later," Tors reports, "we opened Sherman's door. He had four pages of notes in front of him. *Eighty percent* of his notes were correct to a fantastic degree. His notes read:

"'Shoes off foot.

"'The bends, like a diver. Strange boat equipment—human torpedo' (obviously referring to the decompression chamber sequence).

"'Something wrong with apparatus, shooting schedule changed.' (This is exactly what happened when the machine gun jammed.)

"'No, no, not that way. I'll show you! Let me do it!' (This is what I said to the director when I explained to him how the decompression chamber scene should be changed.)

"'Pain, left ear.' (Actually the doctor pricked my right ear.)

"'Communication, sea-to-air.'

"'Divers dropped into ocean and later picked up by helicopter.' (Exactly what happened.)

"'Stuck—back side.' (I was stuck on the back side of the hand.)

"'Underwater explosion of some sort—sound repercussion.' (This obviously referred to our explosive sound signal to call back our divers.)

"This was a very significant evening. Sherman, as he has stated, had not known he was to be tested, as he had been asked to sit in on the investigation of a well-known medium who, at the last moment, failed to appear due to illness. . . . There was no chance for cheating, there was no chance for guessing. Sherman had no way of knowing what had happened to me at sea. I returned from location just in time for the experiment. Sherman did not know anybody in my company or what I was engaged in at that time. A great deal of our shooting was improvised due to weather conditions and other emergencies. Because of a flu epidemic, I had to shoot around my leading man and change plans frequently.

"Among Sherman's many correct impressions, three apparently insignificant words that he scribbled on the first page of his notes were the most meaningful. 'Shoes off foot' didn't mean anything to the observers present, as I did not utter any such words while under hypnosis, but they were firmly etched in my unconscious mind because they referred to an incident with unpleasant connotations, and I still carried bitterness within me.

"During our shooting procedure, I had had a little run-in with our director of photography. It was the first time we had ever exchanged harsh words, and I didn't feel good about it. He had photographed a scene in which the actor was supposed to wear swim fins instead of shoes. After the scene had been photographed, I noticed the actor had worn tennis shoes. When I confronted the camera director in privacy, he assured me that the shoes would not be visible in the frame of the film. I did not accept this explanation and asked him to reshoot the sequence, saying that if he was wrong and the shoes *did* show, it would be too costly to return to the same location for a retake.

"He was so sure of himself that he opposed doing this. Nevertheless, I decided to play it safe and ordered him to reshoot the scene. This he did reluctantly, and there was some tension between us. Unfortunately, there was no way of determining whether the photographer or I was right until the film was developed and projected later.

"The state of tension was still with me during the telepathic experiment that evening. I did not say anything about the 'shoes off' incident while under hypnosis, yet Sherman immediately picked it up and jotted it down on the first page of his notes. No eavesdropping, no spying, no hidden microphones could have given him the information, only the radiation of my subconscious. In fact, no other people who possibly might have mentioned the incident had come in from our shooting location to the city, nor had there been any witness to my heated talk with the camera director.

"Impressed by this, I reanalyzed Sherman's impressions and found that he sensed the things most accurately which emotionally affected me. Machine-gun jamming does not matter much. But when I have to change the shooting schedule, I am upset, because the operation is thrown off balance and a great deal of expense is involved. For a producer to redirect a scene or give instructions to a director is not unusual, but when I said to my very fine director, 'No, no, not that way!' I was upset because for that scene we were on a small boat, and anything I said or did was witnessed by the others."

As Tors himself explained, he was much disturbed by the cameraman's oversight in filming an actor in tennis shoes rather than swim fins. This impression took precedent over any other as I opened my mind to receive and I quickly recorded, "shoes off foot."

I could feel the doctor's shock reaction, and that of the others, as Tors confirmed impression after impression—quite a few of which Tors had not mentioned under hypnosis. The medical doctors looked at one another. Then the leading doctor said: "Very interesting, Sherman. Well, it's getting late. We'd better be getting home. Thank you very much."

And that's all I ever heard!

Happily, an increasing number of medical doctors are taking a professional interest in the manifestations of psychic phenomena, especially in the spiritual healing areas. One of the pioneers in introducing these psychic studies as a part of psychiatric education is the well-known Dr. Stanley R. Dean, president-elect of the American Association of Social Psychiatry.

A questionnaire, sent to deans of medical schools, heads of departments of psychiatry, professors of psychiatry, and psychiatric residents, numbering some 288 respondents, brought replies of over 60 percent favoring the understanding of Psi as important to psychiatric practice.

The authors of a paper urging consideration of this study said in part: "Our profession must expand its horizons to include important fresh dimensions. We submit that Psi is at least one such dimension."

As the originator of a new term, "Metapsychiatry," for the study of Psi, Dr. Dean suggested to members of the American Psychiatric Association that "while some experts advocate the inclusion of a magician on a research team, other notable experts advise against it because of the negative atmosphere it would create, and because of prejudicial results."

A highly sensitive mind can pick up negative thoughts, as in the case of my UCLA experiment. Had I not been conditioned by long years of experience, it could easily have thrown me completely. Prominent actors have sometimes been hit by stage fright when they learn that some person they highly respect or fear is in the audience. The announced intention of magicians to expose psychics as fraudulent—on the assumption that there is no such thing as extrasensory perception—would place many under an emotional strain and defeat any genuine demonstration. No one can be accurate at all times, dependent on different existing conditions. Even radios do not function during bad weather or other forms of interference.

Tors completed his report with the comment:

"Emotional changes that create tension have a great deal to do with adrenaline, and since that evening, Sherman and I have believed that adrenaline plays some part in certain psychic activities. The more cases we studied, the more it seemed that the sender was usually in a highly excitable (adrenergic) condition while the receiver was in a more relaxed (cholinergic) condition—whether awake, in the twilight zone or sleep.

"It is interesting to note that Sherman and I never have lost extrasensory contact. Many times when I have been ill, he has called me on the phone and told me that he felt uneasy about me. His impressions always have been correct. What's more, he has known the nature of my illness."

The reason for my presentation of this case is to assure you at the start that these telepathic powers do exist and can be demonstrated by sensitives like myself who have worked at it for years.

But on occasion, you and everyone has had what you call "hunches," or strong feelings to do or not to do something, or urges to write or call someone you have not had contact with for some time, only to find they were trying to get in touch with you, were ill, had been in an accident, or had some need of help. At the time, you may not have recognized these impressions as different manifestations of your extrasensory faculties. But later you may realize that such impressions could not have been due to your imagination, wishful thinking, or guesswork.

Here now are simple instructions which I have given out to thousands of men and women who have heard my lectures, taken my classes in ESP, or read my self-help books and who have used these techniques to develop their intuitive powers of mind.

For Sending and Receiving Thoughts

1. Relax your body.
2. Make your conscious mind passive.
3. Turn the attention of your conscious mind inward.
4. Imagine a blank, white motion picture screen stretched across the dark room of your inner consciousness.
5. If you cannot easily visualize such a mental screen, let yourself imagine that it is there—as a focal point of attention.
6. When receiving, hold this screen blank. Wait with an inner feeling of faith and expectation that you will see and be able to recognize fleeting mental images from the mind of the individual on whom you are concentrating.
7. When sending, use your imagination to project on this screen mental pictures or strong feelings of that which you wish to communicate.
8. Avoid all efforts to "force," either in receiving or in sending.
9. Usually, the first impression received is the right one. Record it at once, or speak it out—before your conscious mind has a chance to argue you out of it.
10. If you do not succeed in sending or receiving at first, clear your mind and try again. It takes practice to perform ESP, especially if it is an entirely new experience for you.
11. Remember, your subconscious mind, which contains your ESP faculties, is not limited by time or space. Distance is no barrier to thought.

12. In time, if you persist, your ESP powers, functioning through your intuition, can bring you hunches, premonitions, urges to do or not do things, accurate visions or dreams which can guide and protect you in many ways.

Important: Before accepting impressions as genuine, or acting upon them, you must analyze each experience to make sure it is not your fears, worries, wishful thinking, or imagination.

Chapter Four:
How to Recognize and Mentally Handle Different Types of Prospects

"Every individual can be reached and influenced by a different approach, according to his type of personality."

Harold Sherman

Selling is a mental exercise. You need to be on the alert, observationally, as well as intuitively, in evaluating each type of prospect you may encounter. Your success in selling will often depend upon the accuracy with which you are able to classify the individual and treat him accordingly.

We are herewith listing and commenting about thirty-seven different types. There are more, but these will serve to demonstrate that if you hope to hit a high sales score with them, you must play a different sort of ESP game with each one.

Take, for example: The Hard-boiled, "Not Interested, That Ends It," Type, who uses this dodge as a defensive mechanism, but is often a soft touch if approached right.

Some of the toughest customers we have run into are the easiest when we have taken their guff and bounced back with a rejoinder or lighthearted repartee. The first blast of such an individual is designed to blow you out of the ball park. But if you can weather the blow, take it good-naturedly and don't let it get your back up, you will probably sense that beneath this hard-boiled exterior is a person who wants to be recognized and appreciated. It may take several visits, with the blow getting less and less, before you outwind this type and he gives you a chance to say what you tried to say in the first place.

The "Dominating" Type: You don't tell him, he tells you—and if you let him, he sometimes buys.

This type is usually trying to cover up a feeling of inferiority. To do this, he must assume a superior attitude and exercise domination over whomever he can, usually his poor wife. If you give him this satisfaction and don't challenge his feelings of supremacy too much, he may feel sorry enough for you and start buying. Dominating types are rarely basically happy. They know they are not what they pretend to be, and on occasion they try to make up for it by being nice to people.

The "Arguing" Type wants to be convinced, after exchanging about ten thousand words in playing "hard to get."

Give this type the satisfaction of winning a few arguments. To take issue with him too directly will spoil his fun. Follow the trend of his thoughts, and when he is beginning to run out of steam, fire up your own boiler and make a few positive statements about your product or services that you know are irrefutable. Since you have made some concessions, he may now be ready to make some.

The "Know It All" Type likes to show his knowledge by displaying his ignorance. When he's once done so, he's often receptive to being sold.

It takes patience to hear a person like this out, but it can often pay dividends. To show respect for ignorance is a difficult assignment, but if a person doesn't *know* that he doesn't know, he can perhaps be forgiven, to a degree. In any event, attempting to reeducate him, pointing out his errors of thinking, or demonstrating how much you know in comparison, is the wrong way to make a sale.

The "Submissive" Type listens meekly and says little or nothing. He is waiting for you to make up his mind for him.

This is ordinarily an easy type to sell, if you gain his confidence. He is accustomed to being led, but you still have to say the right thing at the right time to hear him say, "That sounds all right. If you feel it will be good for me, I'll take it."

The "Analytical" Type wants to weigh each statement you make—and then act on it—any year. If you have infinite patience, you can land him, because he's usually ready to surrender once he's run out of things to analyze.

Imagine having to live around a man who has to check everything minutely before he accepts it or acts upon it. Such a person wants to know the reason behind everything and what the effect is going to be, before he makes a move or spends a dime. His attitude is, "Don't rush me. I've got to look into this thoroughly. Be sure it's as advertised." Let him look at the labels, test the seams of a suit, challenge the guarantees, until he satisfies himself that you and what you are selling are okay.

The "Think It Over" Type wants to sleep on the proposition while you lie awake, wondering if he will or he won't. You have to wait the opportunity to move in fast for a "closer" before he has time to think.

People who have to mull over things before deciding can be maddening. It's difficult to second-guess them because they themselves don't know where they are going to end up. Best thing to do is let them take their own sweet time. Don't act concerned, let them see that you are confident they will eventually come to the right conclusion—which has to be a purchase of what you have to sell.

The "Show Me" Type wants a demonstration of the product—or ample evidence that it lives up to all the claims for it. He needs the overwhelming treatment to convince.

You might as well load up the ammunition, get your big sales guns ready, set up a demonstration, and put on a display that will really rock him. Then when you see he is properly impressed, call his hand and put a pen in it.

The "Follow the Leader" Type is not so much impressed by the proposition as he is by the names of big buyers. He won't join the parade of previous purchasers unless they are ahead of him.

Nothing impresses a man like this more than "big shots" who are using the product. He thrives on being in such company. He would pay more for a product or a service to be able to say that he is with "the big boys." Show him a list of names and write his name down alongside. That will get him when nothing else does.

The "Independent" Type doesn't give a damn what anyone else thinks—he'll make up his own mind. Give this guy the ball and clear field to the dotted line.

It won't take long for you to discover the prospect who wants to do his own thinking. He will cut you off before you more than get started. "I don't have to hear anything. I know what I want and don't want. No use trying to sell me. How much is this, anyway?"

The "You Can't Sell Me" Type defies you to land him, no matter how good a deal you have to offer. Nothing hurts him more than to have you walk out, without trying. Start to do this and he'll often break down.

Don't take this "can't sell me" attitude too seriously. It's a scare-away for many salesmen who consider such a prospect a waste of time, but all this person wants is a little selectivity and freedom from the barrage of sales approaches. He'll let his buying scepter fall upon the salesman of his choice, if the person is persistent and diplomatic enough.

The "I Hate Salesmen" Type would like you to believe he has a "mad on" against anyone with a briefcase or a "selling look" on his face. Total disregard of this attitude is the best approach, loving him while he hates you.

Prospects like this have probably had unhappy run-ins with salesmen or have been "taken" on bad deals. The mere sight of a salesman or any person who looks like one is enough to spark a conditioned reflex, and start him backing off, muttering: "No, don't try to sell me! I'm not in the market for a damn thing!" Okay, don't try to sell him and he may not love you, but he'll respect you for it—at which point you can begin to make sales progress.

The "I'll Have to Ask My Wife" Type is willing to be sold if you can sell *her*. Lots of times you wonder how she sold him.

This is what you might call a run-around-the-end, or evasive spouse maneuver. He could be a Milquetoast who is afraid to make a decision unless he gets the approval of his wife. Be sure to say nice things about her, and when and if this word gets back to her, it may prove the best selling pitch you could possibly have made.

The "Afraid to Venture" Type likes everything about your proposition but signing on the dotted line. You have to nurse him along and gently place the pen in his hand at the right time.

A little hypnotic influence might not be amiss in dealing with this type. If he was standing beside a swimming pool he'd remain there debating about whether to jump in or not, until someone relieved him of his agony by giving him a good push. Once in the water, once he discovers that it wasn't so bad after all, he dives in by himself. Get this prospect's feet wet with a small deal if possible, and he may take the plunge all the way next time.

The "Putter-Offer" Type would like to keep you coming back, time and again, while he enjoys the sensation of *not* making up his mind. A bird like this needs a sudden, unexpected prod in the rear—and he's hooked before he knows it.

Aggravating is the word for the on-and-off antics of such a prospect. You keep thinking he's going to decide this time, or certainly next time. Well, he can't miss the time after that—but he does! Pick the spot and move in on him. It may get a yes out of him.

The "Kill You With Kindness" Type wants you to sit down and have a drink or a smoke—but gets suddenly busy when you start to make your pitch. He has to be taken off guard with the pitch first—and the drinks and smokes afterward.

As you know, time is money to a salesman, or should be. How much time to invest in a prospect who wants to be too sociable is a worthwhile question. If you have a strong liking for a little drink now and then, you may find yourself heading back to the prospect's address where you know you are going to get something if it is not a sale. Better make him pay for your company with a business transaction before he costs you more than you can afford.

The "Big Front" Type lets you think he's interested in a "big buy" or nothing, and it usually ends up the latter. What he really wants is a small deal, so cross him up by taking him in on any basis you can get him.

The big talkers are usually the small operators. It's

tempting when a prospect begins asking about discounts on a big purchase, but when he tries to hold you to a better price on a smaller buy, this should be all the distress signal you need. Get out of this sales situation the best way you can.

The "Put It on the Line" Type wants the facts in a nutshell so he can give you a quick yes or no. This guy is a fast operator, so don't get in his way or slow him down. Get his yes if possible—and get the hell out of there.

It's a great feeling when you encounter a prospect like this. You save time and money with any deal you can close with him. Cut out any windy approaches, reduce your sales pitch to the minimum, get your order blank ready, and let him supply his own pen. If he's going to buy, he'll have pen to paper almost before you can lay it in front of him.

The "Build You Up for a Let-Down" Type promises you the moon till you eventually end up with a piece of green cheese. Once a guy like this starts his build-up, hit him on the rise.

Have you ever let a prospect sell *you* "castles in the air"? Tell you all the big things he is going to do when he is ready to buy what you have to offer? Just stay with him, it won't be long now. You'll soon be able to cash in on all the time you've spent with him, helping him figure out what he needs. Don't wait for the big payoff. It usually never comes.

The "I'm Too Busy" Type tries to sell you that he can't afford the time for any sales pitch, and takes long enough doing it, for you to have sold *him*. When you run into a bird like this, be just as busy as he is.

Come in like you've only got five minutes to see him—you know he's busy, too—and you're going to give it to him fast. Here's what he needs, here's the price, and here's the place to sign. He probably won't recover until you've left with his order.

The "Evasive" Type makes one appointment after another and breaks them by mistake, *on purpose*. Stay with this baby—you'll wear him out in time.

We knew a man once who not only broke appointments but would make as many as three luncheon dates the same day. He obviously could keep only one, if he kept that. He just couldn't say no to an invitation. If he hadn't been a prominent, influential businessman, he couldn't have gotten away with it, but he had a charming manner and was adept at making apologies. His treatment, however, drove his sales friends crazy . . . all except one. This insurance salesman parked himself in the man's office from early morning until late evening until the prospect ran out of excuses and had to see him. Result: a $100,000 policy.

The "See Me Later" Type likes to dramatize his own importance by keeping a stream of hopeful salesmen calling on him, week after week. Sit this one out—don't leave till he sees you. This will upset his established pattern and leave him wide open for a sale.

It tends to be discouraging when you see a line of salesmen, representing different products and services, in a busy man's office, unable to get an interview. It isn't compensation enough when a sexy secretary gives you the eye and tells you, "Mr. Brown is too busy today . . . but he'll be glad to see you another time. Won't you come back?" The temptation for a little while is to come back to see her—but this routine soon wears thin. Try crashing his private office or catch him on the way in or out. This type often buys when cornered.

The "Plunger" Type takes one listen to your proposition and goes all the way. Pray for more "no problem" prospects like him.

You can usually tell by the glint in your prospect's eye whether or not he will grab like a fish at a wriggling angleworm, as you dangle the contract in front of him. Don't take time to fatten up the bait—when you see he is ready to bite, let him have it. The dots before his eyes will soon form a dotted line. If only there were some more fish like this lucrative fellow!

The ""Take Your Word For It" Type buys what you have to offer strictly on faith in you. Here is an easy touch —and may his tribe increase.

When you find a prospect who buys on faith and couldn't care less about your claims for the product or service, it is time to shout, "Eureka!" Of course it's quite a responsibility when people rely on your word completely, and you'd better be sure this confidence isn't misplaced. If such a prospect is ever disillusioned, he seldom recovers and you have made only a one-time sale.

The "Want to Know All the Facts" Type won't take anyone's word for it. You have to sell this bird with every authority in the book—and affidavits.

Only one thing is good about making a sale to such a prospect. When you have proved the merits of your product, he's so convinced that he usually stays sold. Not only that but you can return and sell him again, with little or no sales resistance.

The "Change His Mind" Type is positive one minute and negative the next until you don't know where you're at—and he doesn't, either. You'll finally have to move in fast on a positive moment and get him before he has a relapse.

In dealing with a prospect of this type, you had better make certain that you are positive when he is negative or you'll lose him altogether. Show him you have confidence that he is going to make up his mind and stay with it. He doesn't really want to be negative—he just can't help himself. He'll thank you when you have added your positiveness to his and pushed him into buying.

The "Nervous, Apprehensive" Type is afraid you are going to sell him despite anything he can do to prevent it. End his tension by doing it!

Fear is a terrible thing and it affects many people. You can sympathize with a person who really needs what you have to sell and yet is afraid it may be the wrong thing and he may later regret having purchased it. Give him every assurance you can. Take his hand and guide it as he writes his name.

The "Sporting" Type will buy your proposition in exchange for a few risque stories worked in as fillers in the "sales pitch sandwich." To do this, you have to know your man.

It always pays to have an assortment of ribald jokes to soften up the prospect if he is the type who likes to hear the latest salesmen's collection. This may go against the grain to stoop to sales in this manner, but human nature is human nature, and there are times when a good story does a better selling job than any sales pitch. When a prospect asks, "Well, what's the latest?" you'd better be ready, because a follow-up sale is not far in the offing.

The "Sell Himself" Type wants you to shut up so he can talk himself into the deal. If you don't, he won't.

Silence is sometimes golden if the salesman can sense when he should button his big mouth and sit tight and let the prospect open his. Occasionally a prospect can tell you more things about the good features your product possesses than you can. In such a case, all you have to do is say "Amen" every few minutes and have the order blank ready for signature when he finishes.

The "Skeptical, Cautious" Type wants to check your personal life, your church affiliation, and your date of birth before he will consider your proposition. Make a clean breast of everything and take his own check.

It beats all how some prospects want to know more about you than they want to know about the product. If you belong to the right church, the right clubs, and the right social group, the product you represent must be okay, so where does the prospect sign?

The "No Money to Invest" Type may be telling the truth and may not. You have to play along with this guy to find out.

It's not so easy to check a prospect's bank account. If you could and did, and he found it out, you'd lose a possible sale. Better take his word for it, but keep calling on him just the same. His financial condition could change, and he'll remember that you never lost your interest in him, even when he told you he couldn't buy.

The "Would If I Had the Money" Type probably is on the level, although you never know. If he gets sold enough, he may suddenly find the money.

Don't write this prospect off. He may have meant what he said, so give him every chance to prove it, when and if he hits a jackpot of one kind or another. Sometimes a prospect's "would-ifs" are a cover-up for a temporarily embarrassed financial status. Be alert to go after him the moment his embarrassment ceases.

The "Who's in This With Me?" Type judges a proposition by who has gone for it. Be sure you mention his friends and not his enemies.

Social status means a great deal to many. If they feel they are buying social status at the same time they are buying your product, they're getting double value for their money.

The "Already Too Loaded" Type may be up to his ears in investments—or may be using this stock statement as a convenient brush-off.

Stay with him and he may permit you to increase his "load." Prospects with money quite often don't know where they stand financially. They stop investing every so often, not because they can't invest anymore, but to take a breather and try to find out where they're at. This is a good spot to catch them in and hit them with another sales pitch. But you have to be sensitive to the right moment to move in.

The "Jump-to-Conclusions" Type is always ahead of your sales pitch, anticipating what you are going to say, with his oft-repeated: "I know! . . . I know! You don't have to tell me!" When you run into this type, hit him with a "closer" before he has a chance to jump back.

It's often disconcerting to run into a prospect who jumps the gun on you and appears to know what you are going to say before you say it. However, the only thing to do is to let him take over. If he wants to do your work for you, so much the better. Sit back, relax, and enjoy it—and save some of your commissions for the little woman at home.

The "Moody" Type never knows what he wants or what's good for him. Find a way to lift his spirits and he'll often want what you have to offer.

You have to be an amateur psychiatrist to handle some prospects. When they are moody or depressed, you have a job on your hands because few people feel like buying when they are mentally and emotionally disturbed. A little sympathy helps, but if you can do something to cheer them up, relieve their tensions, you may relax their purse strings at the same time.

The "Slow-to-Act" Type: You can't push this guy—you have to fit into his rhythm. If you do, you may eventually have him signing a duet with you in the "Sweet Buy and Buy."

It takes a lot of understanding of human nature to make a good salesman. What is considered a good sales pitch alone is seldom enough. Some prospects, like this one, can't be moved by sales eloquence. When they get ready to buy, they will buy—and not until then. Wait them out and you'll be recompensed.

We are sure you have had experience with most if not all the types we have presented. Have you noticed the underlying feeling behind each of these contacts? They have had to be dealt with in a feeling way—you have had to sense how to react mentally and emotionally to each one. Our suggestions, while tinted with some humor, nevertheless contain philosophic pointers. We are confident they have not escaped your attention.

Chapter Five:
How to Size Up a
Person at First Glance
by ESP

"Your total impression of a new acquaintance is the sum total of your five senses plus your sixth sense, relating to the level of feeling."

Al Pollard

Have you ever said to yourself: "Gosh, I sure got off on the wrong foot with that person"? We all have had that experience at one time or another. The question is: Do you know why? . . . And more to the point: What can you do about it to keep it from happening again? The art of meeting people for the first time is just that—an art.

Every day of our lives we are meeting and visiting with new people, some of whom turn out to be good friends. Let me pass along an idea or two that has worked for me.

My office is somewhat larger than most because I have lined it with hundreds of books that I use in my daily work. Also, it is large enough to accommodate ten people in a relaxed meeting environment. Large chairs and an L-shaped couch make for an appealing area for creative thinking.

The door to my office is about ten steps away from my working table and research files. When a visitor comes to see me, I time his or her arrival with my ten steps to the door. As I take those ten steps, I let my conscious mind shift into neutral gear so I can pick up feelings from this new person.

I think of this as "the approach." It's the most important few seconds in the meeting of a new acquaintance—and the most challenging. It may seem simple, but in reality, you are taking the full measure of a person through your five senses plus your sixth sense, the one that knows without experiencing. The quick conclusion you come to can be most helpful if you are right, and unfortunate if you are wrong.

The challenge is to be right . . . to be able to bring into one sweeping glance the following observations plus a personality summation.

In addition to picking up a feeling of the person, here are the key points I observe:

1. *Taste in clothes*: Does this person display conservative or

sporty taste? Tailor-made or off the rack? Is he or she well turned out, or do you get the feeling that clothes are of secondary interest? Are the various garments harmonized in terms of color and material?

2. *Care of clothes*: Would you say this person is careless in dress? Doesn't seem to care if things match up? Clothes look wrinkled and unkempt? Shoes dirty . . . high shine . . . low shine?

3. *Special touches*: If tie has stripes, do they slant from the wearer's right to left or left to right? (The first is American design, the second is British.) If the slant is British, this speaks to a special interest in clothes. If this man is wearing a bow tie, did he tie it or hook it into place? If he is wearing a regular tie, what kind of a knot does he tie and how does the knot fit into his collar?

4. *What about color?* Does this person, man or woman, lean toward warm colors or cool colors? Warm colors usually speak to an outgoing and warm personality, whereas cool colors of blue, gray, muted tones combined with touches of black with white shirts speak to a more conservative person . . . a person who does not take the initiative in a conversation or relationship.

5. *How about hair?* This used to be the main concern of women. Now some men give as much time and energy to their hairstyle as women do. And this tells you a lot. A man with extremely bushy hair is trying to prove something. If his hair is meticulously waved or set with extreme care, the message is clearly one of great pride and reflects the need for being seen with the proper image. Such people are usually rather rigid in their viewpoints, which, like their hair, are fixed in place. By the same token, the man who has a functional haircut and lets his hair reflect the waves or straightness the Good Lord gave him tells us he is willing to be judged by his natural look. Rest assured the message of hair is quite specific. We could do an entire chapter on this subject alone! . . . These broad generalizations can also be applied to hairstyles of ladies and to men and women in wigs!

6. *Complexion is important*: Generally speaking, Caucasian

men and women with dark-skin tend to be more outgoing. They seem to tell you they enjoy the outdoors and do not want to be bothered with details. On the other hand, a person with a pasty complexion seems to reflect a preference for the indoors and probably is not as outgoing in personality, but will respond to detailed concern for any subject under discussion.

7. *Lips have a message*: Thin lips tightly drawn speak to a personality tense and high-strung, whereas full lips usually reflect a more relaxed person. It has always seemed to me that persons with full lips enjoy good food and the material things of life more than thin-lipped people.

   In addition, the natural color of a man's lips (who can tell about the natural color of the ladies'?) can tell you if his circulation is strong and healthy. Lips that are "in the pink" speak of body health. Lips that have a bluish look tell you circulation is weak. Strong and healthy circulation usually reflects a person of vigor and one who enjoys the give-and-take of life. A bluish appearance to the lips tells you a person usually does not want to be rushed in thought or action.

8. *Shape of head is revealing*: I look at the shape of heads to pick up signals as to whether a person places emphasis on thought or on action or on both. As a general rule, I have observed that both men and women who have foreheads that slope at an angle are more action-oriented, whereas those with a vertical forehead line tend to be more thought-inclined.

9. *Chin lines are revealing*: Men and women with large chins usually are active people. If their jawline is very sharp and well defined, you can add determination to the personality mix. If the chin tends to recede, I have found such a person to be reflective and sometimes difficult to work with.

10. *Overall facial configuration*: Men and women with sharp features, thin nostrils, and penetrating eyes are usually very sensitive people whose feelings are easily hurt. They are usually highly intelligent with quick insights. They particularly appreciate special attention. People with

more rounded features, thicker noses, and heavier bone structure seem to be more affable and not quite so sensitive.

11. *Height tells a story*: Height in a man seems to have a bearing on personality. Taller men seem to be less interested in proving their manliness. Shorter men sometimes try to compensate unnecessarily with defensive mechanisms that sometimes make them disliked. On the other hand, a tall woman sometimes feels awkward because of her height. If such is the case, she will often wear low-heel shoes and prefer to sit down when talking with others. However, some tall women will trade on their stature and look down on shorter women—and men. They give the impression they enjoy it. Somehow I doubt it.

12. *Eyes are the window to the soul*: Because the eyes are so closely related to mental images, they are quite revealing. It's always a pleasure to look into sparkling eyes reflecting instant comprehension of what you are saying or doing. You feel that such a person is "with you." I have found that brown-eyed persons are usually warmer in personality and more emotional then blue-eyed men and women. Blue-eyed people seem to be more reserved. Most important, however, is how men and women reflect their emotions through their eyes. I have found that men who have narrow-slitted eyes are more introverted and attendant to details. They seem harder to reach with new ideas. Not many women have eyes like these—thank goodness! Open and well-rounded eyes usually speak to open-mindedness and receptivity. It's delightful to discover a person with twinkling eyes reflecting a rare sense of humor and an appreciation for living. I always feel sorry for those poor souls whose lackluster eyes tell a story of a dull, boring, and uninspired life.

Generalities Are Not Always Accurate

These twelve areas of sizing up people I have just presented simply touch the tip of the personality iceberg.

Most of the personality is not visible to the eye, but these signs do give you a starting point for getting a sharper feeling for a person you are meeting for the first time.

Perhaps your experience in meeting people has been different than mine. If so, fine! Apply whatever observations you feel are dependable through your five senses—before you turn off your analytical mind for a split second to pick up the vibrations the other person is sending your unconscious mind.

It's easy to quickly feel if this new person is sharing or receiving. If sharing is coming toward you as a strong feeling, then respond immediately with appreciation. Let the other person know that you understand his or her message. This appreciation encourages your new acquaintance to open up with more ideas and enthusiasm to share with you. You make such a person feel at ease—instantly.

On the other hand, if this new acquaintance sends you an unspoken message of defensiveness, unsureness, and insecurity, take immediate steps to put such a person at ease. Let him or her know by the way you react that you perceive basic feelings and you are responding in terms of appreciation for psychological needs.

Responding to Psychological Needs

Behavioral scientists generally agree that our conscious mind is our analytical mind. Creative thinking seems to come from the unconscious mind. In other words, our five senses are constantly "programming" our unconscious mind with experiences—both tactile and emotional.

Our unconscious mind, or our computer as some like to call it, stores bits of information from a constant stream of experiences. The Good Lord gave us a computer that makes the mechanical kind look like a toy watch. Unlike the mechanical computers of today, your mind has a creative faculty.

It's your unconscious mind that does the creative work. No scientist knows how—but it works. Remember, the mechanical computer today can tell you "what." It cannot tell you *why*. And it's the "whys" in life that call for creative thinking beyond analytical thought.

In a later chapter I will go into more detail about using your conscious and unconscious minds in creating ideas and events important in your life. For the moment, however, let's concentrate on getting the feelings of a new acquaintance into sharper focus. Our purpose here is to sharpen your ability in meeting people for the first time so that there is a quick rapport. Let me use an actual example I experienced not long ago on the plane trip from New York to Little Rock, Arkansas.

It was a late afternoon flight coming out of La Guardia Airport. For once, I was a bit early and was enjoying reading my *Wall Street Journal*. I was sitting next to the window on the port side of the forward cabin three rows back. The stewardess was busy at her chores getting passengers seated and comfortable.

I was quite happy and relaxed, secure in the fact that I was in the right seat, ahead of time for a change. The aisle seat next to me was vacant. We were scheduled to leave at 5:30 P.M. It was now 5:28, and the stewardess was just about to swing the hatch closed when a hulk of a man came huffing and puffing into the cabin.

She tore off the top of his boarding pass and pointed him toward the seat next to me. All of this I observed over the top of my paper. He swung into his seat and dropped his full weight with a sigh. I could tell he was bushed from hustling through the airport.

"Glad you made it," I said with an offhand observation.

"Yes, so am I," he replied. And that was that. No
more conversation. As frequently happens, our plane was
stacked up on the runway about six planes back before
we could take off. This is always an awkward time in a
plane ride. You feel suspended in time waiting your turn
to leave the earth.

As I sat quietly beside this man weighing at least
250 pounds, I sensed he was an interesting character. In
fact, I got the feeling he was from Europe. So I opened
the conversation to check on that feeling, by stating I was
amazed by the statement in the *Wall Street Journal* that
the Italians were supplying more than 40 percent of shoes
sold in America. This came as no surprise to him. In fact,
he replied quite matter-of-factly that Italian shoes were
very well accepted all across Europe.

This bit of response from him gave me a chance to
hear an accent that triggered me to say:

"What part of France are you from?"

"Normandy," he replied, without realizing he had
said nothing about being from France.

Now that my first feeling was confirmed, I had to
pry a bit more just to satisfy my curiosity about this interesting person.

I went back to reading my paper, but out of the
corner of my eye, I began to study him closer. I could see
his black serge suit was well worn, even a bit slick at the
elbow. I could see a small slipstick (an engineer's ruler)
sticking out of his lapel pocket. I purposely dropped my
paper as if I were looking for something in the pocket on
the back of the seat in front of me. As my eyes glanced
down, I took note of his well-worn black brogans. So as I
continued to hold my paper in a reading position, just for

the fun of it, I nonchalantly asked him what kind of an engineer he was.

"I'm a hydrological engineer," he replied quite easily, still not reacting to my two "hits."

For some reason, I made a comment that the Ohio River had recently flooded and created a unique backwater situation. "It seemed to me," I observed casually, "the recent news on the damage in the Ohio River Valley reflects on the engineering accuracy of the shoreline created at the top of the flood pool."

For a second, my friend was quiet. Then he leaned forward and looked me in the face. "Strange you should say that," he said. "I'm on my way to an Ohio court on that very point. Are you an engineer?" he asked.

"No. I just happen to be interested in water resources and how we manage them in America."

We both became quiet for thirty minutes or so. Then I probed again. "Have you ever built hydro dams?" I asked with obvious interest in my voice.

"Yes," he said with a bit of distance in his voice. I could tell I had struck a sensitive nerve of some kind. I became quiet waiting on his further statement. "It was in Korea," he said rather flatly. "In fact, that's where I met my wife. She was a native there. We've been married six years."

I could sense a note of sadness in his tone. So to follow up a new feeling, I asked: "Are you headed for Little Rock?" He replied, "Yes." It was then that I made my last psychic observation for a final confirmation of my feelings.

"You know," I said tentatively, "Arkansas is a state where you can get a ninety-day divorce if you can prove residency for that period of time."

"Yes, I know about that. I am meeting my wife at

the airport. She has been living in Arkansas now for ninety days."

And that was the end of our conversation. Since he didn't seem interested in discussing the subject further, I felt I was beginning to pry.

Shortly, our plane landed in Little Rock. He gathered up his hat and overcoat the stewardess brought him. During that interval of landing, he did not offer one word of conversation, so I remained quiet also.

I walked out behind him in the aisle and watched him go straight to a small woman waiting for him. They shook hands and walked off together . . . he bulking tall above her, and she a rather petite figure of a woman walking quickly beside him.

"There," I said to myself, "go two unhappy people."

Meeting People for the First Time Can Be an Exciting Experience

Through the years of traveling across our great country, I have developed a "kneejerk" reaction to meeting new people.

Usually when I am to conduct a seminar or make a speech in a city away from home, a person meets me at the airport and escorts me to the hotel. Since it is my strong desire to give of my very best, I begin by tuning in the person meeting me.

My "knee jerk" reaction makes an instant visual evaluation of the basic factors just described. This analysis begins the moment I determine who my host or hostess is to be. It's better to perceive a person from head to toe and then gradually walk closer to pick up a more detailed sensation.

I purposely use the word *sensation*. The feeling you experience as you approach a new acquaintance is most important—if you are concentrating on being aware in every detail.

My own system is to make the first distant observation quickly with my conscious mind. Then as I approach the person closer, I try to let my conscious mind shift into "neutral gear" so that my subconscious mind can pick up a feeling at a sixth-sense level.

This may sound like a lot of unsupportable abracadabra, but all I can say is that it works for me. By the time I actually shake hands with this new person, I have a distinct readout, as my computer friends say.

From the time I make my first connection with this person meeting me at the airport until we arrive at my hotel, I check and double check first impressions to get on target. My conversation might go something like this:

"I get the feeling you are a professional in the field of communication." This observation is based upon the feeling this person is outgoing and quite at ease with people.

"You might say that," my new friend replies. "I take pride in being a professional salesman. I guess that makes me a communicator."

"Of the highest order," I respond with enthusiasm.

Right off the bat, I have gained this person's interest. By letting him or her know that I appreciate a special talent, I follow up with enthusiasm to project respect for the status of a professional salesman. This reflects acceptance and admiration of a talent and a profession.

Then I continue with: "I get the feeling you are selling an intangible service rather than tangible products. Would that be a fair assumption?"

"Yes," comes the quick reply, "I sell life insurance."

Now all of my first impressions begin to relate. It is

time now to move into a specific area of the other person's self-interest—the SI Factor, I call it.

"Tell me, do you prefer selling ordinary life policies to young marrieds rather than group insurance to companies?"

The feeling for this question comes from my observation that this person is a one-on-one salesperson rather than a mass producer. In other words, this person has a warm feeling for people as individual personalities.

This question stimulates my new friend in great depth as to why it's more fulfilling to sell young marrieds a life insurance program. From then on, as we get to know each other in more detail, it's all downhill.

My questions continue to probe deeper into my new friend's self-interest. By the time we arrive at the hotel, we have established a warm rapport. As I shake hands and express appreciation for being met at the airport, the conversation usually goes like this, with the other person speaking first:

"I'm really looking forward to hearing your presentation tonight! . . . I know all our members in the club will enjoy hearing you as much as I have enjoyed talking with you."

All of which is to say that because I cared enough to sense . . . to feel . . . and to relate, my new friend and I developed mutual interests, making the world a more interesting place for living and experiencing.

I call this the workings of Self-Interest Dynamics!

Chapter Six:
How to Tell in Advance What a Person Is Going to Say or Do

"Reading the mind is really sensing the transmitted feelings of others and putting them into words."
Harold Sherman

Often you have been about to say something when your wife—or husband or friend or business acquaintance or stranger to whom you are talking—starts to say the same thing. You may put it down to coincidence or happenstance and leave it at that without realizing the significance of this quite ordinary occurrence.

Actually, you were tuning in on another's thoughts —either that, or the other person was tuning in on yours.

Sometimes you may not be getting the exact words, but you are expressing how another person is feeling at the moment in words of your own.

This is a form of mind-to-mind communication in its most primitive sense. Perhaps before language was developed, early man functioned largely on the feeling level which he illustrated by making signs or drawing crude pictures to convey his desires to others.

It may well be that all other animals and forms of life have their own communication systems, all related to feeling—an instinctive reaction to their environment and experiences.

Quite often, what individuals say is not what they're really thinking. They may be saying no when they mean yes or vice versa. It is worth reemphasizing that feeling is the universal language. When one's true feelings can be sensed, regardless of what may be said, you can always depend on them.

, A shocked and highly disturbed father contacted me recently about his sixteen-year-old son, a star high-school athlete who had come home "plastered." When his parents reprimanded him, he let out a bitter blast at them, declaring it was all their fault, that they weren't really interested in what happened to him, didn't care whether he lived or died, so "to hell with you and everything."

"I never heard such abusive language," the father said. "It was as though he let loose a lifetime of pent-up resentment of us. He laid it on the line, and his mother and I couldn't do anything but stand there and take it. We could begin to see now what we have done wrong in our relations with our son, who really is a fine boy. But how are we going to regain his respect and regard?"

The parents were wealthy people. They were active in what is called high society, always on the go at fashionable dinners and cocktail parties, taking in the horse races and all manner of social events. They were seldom at home, giving the son all the money he needed, getting him out of the way, as he accused, so they didn't have to pay much attention to him. They applauded his sports achievements and took a passing interest in his academic standing, just so a son of theirs "lived up to the family name," but he seldom saw them from week to week and rarely on a personal basis. His parents were always "too busy." This had been going on for years, and finally he couldn't take it any longer.

As he looked back, the father told me, he should have detected tell-tale signs of a growing disturbance in his son, but he hadn't been "reading" him right—the son had always been deferring to his parents and their "plans" for him without protest, apparently suppressing any desires or needs of his own so as not to interfere with their activities—in other words, to "keep out of their way."

"His mother and I were so absorbed in our own doings, which had taken priority over our interest in our son, that we had left him shift pretty much for himself," said the father. "We were appalled at our realization of what we had unwittingly and thoughtlessly done. We had taken for granted that if we provided all the physical things our son might need, he could take care of himself, live his own life, and we could be free to live ours. Now we know—we hope not too late—how much our boy really means to us and how shallow and actually meaningless our round of dinners and cocktail parties and social activities is in comparison. What can we do about it?"

To restore a feeling of confidence in a person is not easy, especially in a young son or daughter, who will naturally wonder if a parent is just pretending to care. A real change in attitude must be contained in deeds, not words.

Family eruptions like this, all too frequent today, may have touched your homelife at one time or another. In any event, it is well that you learn how to "read" the real feelings of members of your family, to determine what their actual thoughts, desires, fears, apprehensions, and resentments may be.

Be sure that you are not taking those close to you at home or in business for granted. The more you can sense their real feelings toward you and others, the happier, more successful relations will exist. Changing conditions can bring about changing attitudes of mind and heart that can always be communicated if these feelings can be properly sensed and interpreted.

This doesn't mean that you have to go about wondering all the time what people are thinking about you. I have received many letters from people complaining that they are being dominated by the thoughts of others, that they can tell what is on their minds, that they just know some people have it in for them. And how can they protect themselves from the evil influences around them?

It is true that you are surrounded by an ever-changing sea of thought vibrations—and that at times, depending on your emotional state, you can tune in on like feelings from the minds of others, especially those with whom you are closely associated. We seldom recognize the sources from which like feelings come, to which we are momentarily attuned, but we are influenced by them to a degree. The only way to demagnetize yourself, when any of your disturbed feelings have become attuned to the disturbed feelings of others, is to take command of your mind and let go of such feelings.

For years, I have followed a little meditative practice of sitting quietly at night, reviewing my day's activities, and trying to see myself as others may have seen me. I have asked myself if I might have given a better account of myself in thought, conduct, and action. Invariably, I have found room for improvement. If I am aware of anything I have done that may have been displeasing to others or anything they have done that has been offensive to me, I try to eliminate any ill feelings so I don't have anything in my consciousness to attract similar experiences in the future.

Seldom do we take the time to relax in anything we are thinking or doing. Much is to be gained by being a good listener. We often pay too little attention to others when they are talking. If you do, you can read between the lines of what they are saying and gain more intuitive knowledge of what they really have in mind.

Take inventory of yourself. Have you formed a cover-up habit of not expressing how you really feel about many things for fear you will not be understood—or that others may take issue with you? Are you bound by conventionality, by religious, racial, or other prejudices, so that you are walking on "mental eggshells" most of the time in your relations and dealings with others—so that few people, if any, actually feel that they know the real you?

If you don't open up to others, how can you expect them to open up to you? The way life is being lived today, many people are emotionally tense, fencing with each other, not meaning half they say and tending to be suspicious of almost everyone rather than trusting.

What a person is saying is one thing, but what that same person is feeling at that moment is often another. The next idea he is about to express in words is forming from feelings in his subconscious. At this point, if you are relaxed and paying close attention, you can intercept these feelings and interpret them before they emerge into words.

What you are actually doing is listening to the voice, hearing what is being spoken, and at the same time sensing the next thoughts prior to their utterance. This is not difficult to do. You will be surprised, when you try it, how much success you can attain in anticipating what is on a person's mind before he speaks it. You can also improve your reception of feelings that he is restraining himself from expressing, for diplomatic, personal, or other reasons.

These extrasensory faculties are all a part of your mental equipment, ready to be used when you have learned how to apply them. They will bring you information in mental imagery or feeling form, direct from the subconscious of the conscious or unconscious sender. If some people feel a need to reach you and cannot get you by phone, their strong feelings of urgency may transmit an energy that causes you to think of them and to take the initiative, either writing or phoning to see what's on their minds. Sending and receiving can be a two-way street, and it is sometimes difficult to tell which one thinks of the other first.

If you are a cat or dog lover, you can practice communicating with your pets on the feeling level. After a time they can understand what you mean by certain words. Even though they can't speak in return, they will show you what they want and they will accept or reject whatever you offer until they get what they want. We have two cats, Dixie, a male, and Lady, who understand us better than we understand them. When they need to get our attention, they will line up, silently, side by side, and point with their heads to their dishes or the door and give us the stare, until we ask: "What is it? What do you want?" Then they will either run to the door or go to where we keep their food and say, without words, "Can't you see? This is it!"

We give our cats the run of the house, so nothing is sacred to them. We are as apt to see them on top of a high shelf, or hidden away on top of a box of book manuscripts, or under the television set, or on my desk, nosing me to be petted and lying on my scripts or trying to get in on the telephone conversation when the phone rings nearby, or getting on the foot of our bed, or on our laps when the day's work is done and we are relaxing in the living room.

This is all communication of a sort. We don't try to make our cats do anything not natural to them . . . and they feel they have as much right to our home as we do. Actually, the secret of happy living is the ability to have the right feeling toward all living things, difficult as this often is to do. We speak of "man or animal," as though we are not animals ourselves. But we are endowed with a higher type of consciousness—and in my opinion we endeavor to live up to our actually unlimited potential.

Chapter Seven:
How to Attune
Yourself to an
Individual's Personal
Needs and Wants

*"By becoming acutely aware of
another person's feelings, you can
sense psychological needs and
material wants."*
Al Pollard

Having spent my entire life in the field of writing, advertising, and marketing, I always think in terms of fulfilling needs—that is, until one evening, years ago, I had a long discussion with a clinical psychologist friend who convinced me that my approach was limited. I maintained that in advertising the objective was to fill obvious needs with products or services. The better you could identify needs, the more success you could have in selling.

"No," he said, "that is not true. What you are doing is selling to material wants. You are not pinpointing psychological needs. That's where basic selling really begins.

"Psychological needs come first," he continued. "Needs are then expressed in terms of material wants. So, if you are really appealing to people, you must first establish these psychic needs. Then project your product or service in terms that fulfill needs first and material wants second."

So it was, many years ago, I became deeply interested in the psychological needs of people. It has been an exciting voyage into the psyche of men and women, both young and old. In fact, that voyage has taken me to the root stem of existence from the hour of birth until the moment of death.

No two people have the same psychological needs.

Picking up these psychological shades of differences is an art—not a science. There is no way to avoid generalities. Yet, by being acutely aware of other people and their special personality traits, it is possible to pick up psychological needs and material wants.

The basic area we are considering is the individual's reflected feelings. As Harold Sherman has maintained for years, feeling is the basis for all communication.

For instance, if you say to your wife, "You know, you have a face that would stop a clock," you can begin ducking. But on the other hand, if you say with warm feeling: "Darling, when I look at you, time stands still," that's a different story! The idea was about the same, but the words and the feeling were quite different . . . and so is the reaction!

Let's consider now how you go about attuning yourself to an individual's personal needs and wants.

To begin with, let's agree that no matter what level a person has attained intellectually, feeling still dominates communication. In addition, there are basic emotions that relate to deep-seated wellsprings of personal concern.

Behavioral scientists agree that the following three psychological needs are common to just about everyone:

First, there is the desire of understanding one's personal identity.

Second, we find the need for stimulation.

And third, a strong desire for security.

These three areas cover many subareas that are important to each individual. Let's take the first psychic need in depth . . . self-identity. In dealing with seminar groups I have found that most everyone *wants to be somebody*! There's nothing new in that idea, but it is one of the strongest building blocks in dealing successfully with people at the feeling or psychic level. Too often, in wanting *to be somebody ourselves*, we keep pushing our viewpoints instead of bringing out and listening to the other person's.

This lack of awareness and lack of feeling for the other person's aspirations blocks the effective working of our sixth sense. We get so inner-directed in all we think and say that we fail to pick up personality signals coming toward us at a subvocal level.

Nothing is more sensitive to an individual than his or her own perception of the image he or she projects to others. Frequently, individuals are aware that the image they wish to project is not the one coming back to them from their friends or new acquaintances.

This personal frustration does interesting things to people. Frequently, a man or woman tries to compensate for this loss of image by overreacting. When people are doing this, they act defensively—whether they know it or not.

In other words, they are telegraphing their need for being appreciated. They want to be liked in the worst sort of way. They want to "belong," as the saying goes. So ask yourself constantly: "Am I helping someone *to be¯ somebody*?"

I am thinking of a young man who once worked in our organization. He was aggressive, intelligent, but dedicated to the wrong personal concepts. His philosophy seemed to be: "Do unto others before they do unto you!" He could have gone far in our company, but he turned out to be his own worst enemy.

His early childhood was such that it made him need extra appreciation from others. He would do just about anything to get that appreciation.

Whenever his shortsighted actions got clients mad, he immediately began looking for someone to blame. He just couldn't face the fact he had goofed. His desire *to be somebody* created a fragile personality that could not meet the test of truth—because it would damage the image he had himself. He didn't know it, but he was overreacting to threats to his image. So he became highly defensive in his thoughts and actions. His career with our company was cut short because he had this blind spot in his personality. Perhaps he will learn to discard his phony set of values: "The end always justifies the means. People do not respond warmly when treated by the Golden Rule. It's the Brass Rule that pays off faster!"

Chapter Eight:
How to Maintain Your Mental and Emotional Control So As Not to Short-Circuit Your ESP Powers

"Uncontrolled emotions can prevent the dependable functioning of your extrasensory power."

Harold Sherman

Hundreds of letters come to me from emotionally sensitive people who have picked up impressions from others or have had visions or dreams of a coming event or have imagined dire things happening to them or loved ones, wanting to know how to control such feelings.

Quite often they have expressed a desire to control these higher powers of mind so they can distinguish the difference between a genuine impression and a false one, usually dictated by their fears or worries. Once a premonition of a possible tragedy has come true, they are afraid they may get more sensings of deaths or injuries to friends and relatives, if not themselves. And how can they keep from getting these kinds of feelings?

"Am I creating the very things I don't want to have happen?" some have asked. "I'm getting so I'm afraid to have a negative thought. I wish I wasn't so sensitive to things around me. I either want to get control of this ESP thing or get it out of my mind entirely."

Once a person has undergone what he knows, beyond any doubt, to have been a true psychic experience, however, no one can tell him that these powers do not exist. What is immediately baffling and a bit unnerving is the realization that these spontaneous telepathic or precognitive experiences cannot be reproduced at will. They flash into consciousness, out of a clear sky, as it were, taking precedence over any ordinary thoughts at the moment, and leaving such an unmistakable image or impression of certain knowledge as to defy dislodgement. The receiver cannot argue himself out of the feeling that something has happened or will happen and he or she is relieved only when some confirmation or verification of this extrasensory adventure is obtained.

If something like this has happened to you, possibly you have told few people, if any, about it for fear of ridicule or the suggestion that you may be in need of psy-chiatric treatment. Perhaps you have never had a recognizable experience of your own, but have always been interested in ESP and have hoped that you might have an exchange of thought impressions from or about some friend or loved one.

It has long been my contention that everyone possesses the faculty of extrasensory perception in more or less undeveloped form. The reason these higher powers do not function repeatedly, if at all, has been due largely to our schooling; the still-prevalent belief that we are limited by our five physical senses and that any other form of mental phenomena can be explained away as imagination, hallucination, obsession, or a form of schizophrenia. Children who display unusual sensitized awareness, who seem to know what is going on beyond the reach of their ordinary senses, or who have invisible playmates, have often been punished by their parents or told that they mustn't think those kinds of thoughts and must stop their wild imaginings.

We often fear and condemn what we do not understand. The unknown, in any area of life, is usually feared, and nothing more pronouncedly than any mysterious workings of the mind.

The average businessman or layman will probably feel more comfortable if you talk to him in terms of the "intuitive powers." This is a more acceptable term and a safer psychological approach. Students can be taught how to develop their intuitive faculties without having to admit that they are actually dealing with the extrasensory realm.

At a time that gold was selling for around $200 an ounce, a sizable investor who had been looking to me for "intuitive guidance" in his business dealings for the past several years could not believe me when I told him that I had a definite impression it would go up to more than $800.

"If I could depend on that prediction, I could make a fortune," he said. "I've followed many of your 'hunches' with profit, but this is just too fantastic."

When it really happened, he phoned me that it was one of the economic regrets of his life that he had talked himself out of taking advantage of my intuitive flash.

"You've told me that you can't always be right," he said. "You have never made any claims at hundred percent accuracy, but time and again, you have had correct impressions, seemingly against the trends or market expectations. I should have remembered this and gambled on it. A hundred thousand invested in gold could have brought me three or four times that amount. I've taken chances before. Why didn't I do it this time?"

I explained to him that the conscious mind is limited in its knowledge or awareness. It will always try to argue a person out of any "hunches" or urges that come from the subconscious.

"I know," he said. "I debated about making a large purchase of gold, but the more I thought about it, the more my conscious mind tried to tell me that gold couldn't go anywhere near that high and that I would probably lose my shirt. So I finally decided that this was one time when you couldn't be right and that I had better stay out of the gold market. Where in the world did you get this feeling or information?"

"This is a question I've never been able to answer," I replied. "When people come to me with a problem or a situation they are facing and ask what impressions I may get about it, I let my mind 'wonder' what might or could happen out of the existing circumstances. Usually images begin to flash across the screen of my mind, or strong feelings come to me, which I put into words. I have to keep my conscious mind out of this while I am doing it. If I let it interfere by trying to tell me, 'This couldn't be true, you are just imagining things,' it will stop the flow of impressions and I will lose contact with this extrasensory power manifesting on my subconscious level."

The investor said: "I have been trying to train my mind to do for me what your mind is doing for you . . . but I guess I am too close to my problems, I don't have faith I can get dependable direction, so I keep coming to someone like you."

"That's the trouble with many people," I pointed out. "They spend millions of dollars a year seeking guidance from psychic counselors, fortunetellers, astrologers, tea readers, mediums, and so-called masters, instead of making the effort to learn how to develop and use their own ESP powers. You've seen me demonstrate, time and again, so you know these powers actually exist. I never insist on your following the impressions I give you, only to analyze them in the light of your own experience, and then make your own decisions."

"I know," said the investor. "It sounds easy—but so often your impressions are so different from what seem to be known facts that I just can't make myself believe them. But when I *have* acted on your advice, I've more often than not had good results—far better than what would have been my own judgment—so can you blame me for coming back to you when I feel a strong enough need?"

No question about it—when you have found you can rely upon someone to give you information of value, it is a great temptation to go to him or her rather than trying to follow your own intuition. In this rapidly changing world, so much is riding on right or wrong decisions that it is difficult for most of us, who may be under different economic and social and personal pressures, to control mind and emotions. It is generally true that when you are disturbed, you are in no condition to call upon your higher powers of mind for guidance. You are apt to be picturing through fear or worry what you don't want to have happen, blocking out any possibility for your intuition to show you a way out.

In my case, in the thousands of impressions I have given out during my life, I always feel a sense of great responsibility to the individual seeking help. After I have written or spoken these impressions, I am often tormented by the speculation of my conscious mind that they might be wrong, cause unwarranted grief or concern, or useless search efforts where missing persons, planes, and animals are involved.

The fact that I have never charged for whatever services I could render has freed me from any feelings of obligation or any economic compulsion to "produce results." I have no motivation other than to be helpful. I always make clear that I cannot assure accuracy. I can only tell the party seeking aid what I feel, regardless of whether the impressions appear to be good or bad, correct or incorrect, in part or in whole.

Often, after I have conveyed my impressions, people seeking help do not write or inform me whether or not these impressions have been right. I am always left with a wonderment of how accurate I may have been, if at all, which gives me a feeling of "unfinished business." Then there are times when people I have helped in years past run into another problem and write seeking aid again, finally confirming what I did for them before.

Here is a current example from a Mr. H.B. of McKean, Pennsylvania, who wrote: "I communicated with you some years ago while living in Indiana, and you were of some help to me. I was about to take a flight to

Chicago for a business meeting. For some reason, I had a deep fear of that flight. Here is what you told me when you phoned me: 'I foresee a little rain but a smooth flight.'

"Well, as it turned out, it rained, but through the rain, it was one of the smoothest flights I've had. Strangely enough, no turbulence!

"Now I am about to embark on another flight into New York City next week and, again, I am uneasy, perhaps because of the rash of DC-10 disasters currently. Do you feel any adverse vibrations whatever to my flight next week?"

His letter did not arrive in time for me to contact him, but I had a feeling the flight would be uneventful—and I am sure it was. If Mr. H.B. had been able to put aside his fears, project his mind imaginatively into the future, and ask this higher power within the same question he was asking me, he could have received the same reassurance. But so long as he was emotionally uneasy, any thoughts that might have come from his subconscious would have been colored, perhaps reflecting his disturbed feelings.

Usually, when you need a specific answer to a serious problem, you are under pressure of the circumstances and find it difficult, if not impossible, to clear the conscious mind of its apprehensions so that you can withdraw its attention from the outer world and make contact with the subconscious so that your ESP powers can function.

Given an open channel to the inner conciousness, one could see, as I foresaw, "a little rain but a smooth flight." In some miraculous way, the answers are there, if we can only set the stage to receive and recognize them!

In all my books, I have emphasized in one way or another how imperative it is for those who would like to

· develop their extrasensory powers to aim for the acquirement of emotional stability. Without reasonable control of your emotions, it is possible to open your mind to influences that will give you wrong answers and even mislead and misguide you.

There are times when I do not feel up to making my mind receptive and trying to receive impressions. I never attempt to force these ESP powers to function. If I do, I am apt to activate my imagination or my wishful thinking, and they will color whatever I may bring through. There is a difference in feeling when a genuine impression is manifesting. You can learn to recognize it and go with it when such a feeling comes. But the moment this feeling begins to change or you sense your conscious mind seeking to enter in and embroider your mental imageries, shut it off entirely! Blank your mind, and begin over again.

With a little experience, you will begin to look forward to selected times a day when you can get off by yourself, relax, review any problems you may have, and pass them on to your subconscious so it can go to work on them and let your extrasensory faculties, functioning like a computer, bring you the answers you must have. They will often flash into your consciousness as though someone has turned on a light. Inspired by this self-illumination, you will then see clearly how to proceed.

Chapter Nine: How to Know When to Sell—and When Not to Sell

"When you have thoroughly appealed to the wants and needs of a prospect and have built up enthusiasm, that's the time to be quiet and let the buying desire take over."

Al Pollard

One of the greatest talents in the art of selling ideas, services, or products is getting the prospect to tell you his or her reason for buying.

It doesn't just happen. It occurs because you, the idea initiator, make it happen. You make it happen through the skillful blending of awareness, an understanding of the psychic needs and material wants, and the feeling you pick up at the sixth sense level.

All master salesmen have this ability. It has been my observation that professional salesmen have an uncanny feeling for people. They enjoy being around them. They enjoy the give-and-take of kidding around and swapping stories and experience. In other words, they are outgoing people with a keen sense of awareness for their fellowmen. Perhaps they don't even understand why they are so successful.

Yet on the other hand, I have known top-ranking salesmen who did not have this outgoing mannerism. But, being leaders in their field, they knew when to stop selling and start listening to the prospect telling them why they would buy whatever was being sold.

They had a sixth sense for relating to the feeling level of others. They also can apply this feeling information in relating accurately to the self-interest of the person being sold.

My first lesson in this approach to selling came to me when I was about ten years old. My father was a wholesale dry-goods salesman, and he gave me many wonderful tips on how to get an order.

In the summertime I used to haul his sample cases in and out of the stores he was calling on. On the weekends we would return to the store that bought a large order and hold special sales to help move the goods.

One particular store was in the center of a large black population, and Saturday was always a heavy business day. In addition, our special sales attracted even more customers. I thought it would be easy to sell these customers because there were so many of them wanting to buy. I found out it wasn't that simple, however. Time after time, I gave what I thought was a good presentation of a particular item but failed to make a sale.

This bothered me because I was using all of the suggestions my father had given me. I finally discovered I was giving too much information that wasn't particularly needed—or wanted. And I was pushing too hard for the sale. That was the real key: I was pushing too hard. Also, it finally dawned on me I needed to relate what I was trying to sell to the needs and wants of each prospective customer.

I shall long remember my first ESP sale! A rather stout mother indicated she wanted some clothes for her six-year-old son, who was just starting school. Her attention was drawn immediately to a sailor suit I had displayed. It had the typical sailor's collar, and there were stripes on the left sleeve just like regulation sailor suits. Best of all, it had a braided cord that went around the collar and looped into the upper breast pocket with a boatswain's whistle. And for mama, that did it.

"Oh, look, George," she exclaimed with enthusiasm, "this is the perfect suit for your first day at school!"

George said nothing. He obviously didn't want a sailor suit. I got a sixth sense feeling from him that he felt it would make him look like a sissy, but he couldn't go against his mother. So I sided with George. It did look like too much for your first day at school when you didn't know what to expect. But I realized if I was to make this sale, I would have to sell mama.

For the first time in my life, I projected myself into the feelings of another to get a viewpoint. It seemed clear to me she was concerned about making her George look like a little man, since he was rather small for his age.

That was my clue—help her make George look

manly. So I made a suggestion. "How would you like to have George look like a leader?" I could see that the idea struck home, because she was giving thought to my suggestion before she replied.

"Well," she said, "I thought the sailor suit would make George stand out like a leader because he would look so different."

"That could be. But why don't we find some clothes that make George actually *feel* like a leader?"

"What do you have in mind?" she asked quickly.

I thought for a moment and then replied out of instinct for George.

"Let me show you a dark brown pair of corduroy long pants and a sports shirt to match." As I said this, I looked at George to check his reaction. I could see I struck pay dirt. Again, I was trying to project myself into needs and wants, although at the time I didn't know this was what I was doing.

George's mother also took a reading on George and saw he was liking the idea. So off we went to the pants and shirt department. Whereupon I learned a valuable lesson in selling. Not once did I mention the quality of the fabric or the tailoring or any other product specific. All I did was to continue building the image of George looking like a leader in those corduroy long pants and a jazzy sports shirt I had selected.

Needless to say, I made the sale. Mama was happy. George was happy, and I was happy. One more thing I learned: When I saw that mama was buying the idea of her son looking like a leader, I became silent and let her begin to get the feeling of this concept. Then she began to tell George how much he was going to look like a leader. . . . She was selling me!

I had learned my lesson on talking too much—about the wrong thing.

Years ago, I had the pleasure of dining with Elmer Wheeler, who had just finished speaking to our Sales and Marketing Club. As you may recall, Elmer was the man who coined the idea of "Don't sell the steak, sell the sizzle!" Which is another way of saying: "Don't sell the product, sell the benefits."

That visit with Elmer Wheeler got me to thinking. All salesmen are trained to sell the benefits, yet many never learn that lesson. But as I thought about this basic idea, it kept coming to me that the real key was knowing *which* benefits to sell to a specific prospect.

There's nothing new in that thought. What is new is how you determine which benefit to project to a prospect quickly to get his or her interest. And that's where sixth sense selling comes into the picture.

So, it became clear to me that my psychology friends were right on the target when they said to me: "Al, you've got to appeal to psychic needs and material wants."

I can't emphasize this point too much. It is the key to all successful selling, day after day. And yet, I am not aware of many sales training programs that go into this subject in any great detail. Intuitive selling seems to be a bit much for many sales leaders, even though these leaders are using this system—and don't realize how good it is!

Those of us who have spent a lifetime in the field of marketing and selling have a great respect for the idea that *professional selling is an art*! And the more you learn and know about selling, the greater you respect this statement.

Red Motley, dean of selling and a former publisher of *Parade* magazine, the Sunday newspaper supplement, made his saying famous that gave me much new enthusiasm for my sixth sense selling. Red used to tell the sales world, "Nothing happens until somebody sells something!" And, "You never hear the sales talk that sells you!"

That last statement—"You never hear the sales talk that sells you"—is the one that convinced me that sixth sense selling is the key to learning the art of professional selling.

And the reason is simple. A professional salesman is highly skilled in talking about *you* and *what's important to you!* The quicker he can zero in on you and what's important to you, the quicker he can generate the buying impulse based upon psychological needs and material wants.

Experience tells us that every sale is different, just as every person is different. This is why selling by the law of averages in making calls is very old hat. Nothing is more monotonous than having to listen to a sales pitch that's been memorized and stated with corporate precision.

I recall insurance salesmen who used to call on me back in the thirties and forties. They had lots of enthusiasm. They had their sales talk down pat. In those days all they could think of was selling me an ordinary life policy with a twenty-year pay feature, meaning I could collect a lump sum after paying premiums for twenty years. I can still hear these salesmen comparing their policy to policies of other companies, thereby showing me what a good deal they had.

The salesmen who left me colder than a flounder in the Deepfreeze were the ones who opened up their talks saying their company was having a sales drive because on the 26th of the month, the company president was having his birthday and everyone was working extra hard to meet their birthday quota. The implication was that I should join in this festive occasion by buying a twenty-year pay policy as my way of saying "Happy Birthday!" to the president. Needless to say, I never bought an insurance policy on that basis.

In those days, the accepted sales procedure was for the insurance agent to make fifteen calls, to get three interviews, to make one sale. This was the calling code agents lived by. And I must say it worked because in the skinny thirties, the insurance companies of America had all of the money corralled.

Today, this sales approach has taken a 180-degree turn. Today's insurance salesman is a specialist. He or she knows how to prospect with greater insight toward making the sale. Today's insurance salesperson is using his or her sixth sense to relate much closer to psychic needs and material wants.

No longer does a man without a job become an insurance agent, sell his best friends, and then leave the business. Quite the contrary. Agents today are highly trained to relate their special policies to special needs and wants.

This is particularly true of the big producers in the insurance profession. They are the agents who sell million-dollar policies in a highly specialized approach.

I recall reading in *Fortune* magazine about one of these highly specialized professionals. In one particular case, he researched a certain prospect's needs for three months. By whatever means he had, he secured inside information as to this wealthy prospect's insurance coverage. After exhaustive research, he found the weak spot he was searching for. This gave him his opening.

Now that he was properly armed with a specific proposal based upon this prospect's glaring need, he managed to get an interview with this extremely busy executive on the promise that he needed only five minutes.

He kept his date and he kept his word. In less than five minutes, he convinced this big-time executive that he knew more about his life insurance coverage than he did. . . . He played his trump card as to the man's need. Right there on the spot, the prospect signed the application for a million-dollar policy. But that's not all. The agent then had to get the executive checked by a doctor, and with a big-time executive, that's never easy.

So what happened? The usual, and the unusual. The executive said he just didn't have time this week, but perhaps next week. Whereupon the agent, closing in for the kill, told the executive not to bother about next week. He had a doctor standing by in the waiting room and could get the examination over in ten minutes. And so he did!

This true story is a classical example of relating first to a psychic need. The executive wanted complete security, which he thought he had, but found out he didn't. And second, he wanted plenty of money to meet his material wants.

The insurance agent was smart enough to realize this approach and hung his entire sales presentation involving months of research on these two points. And even more important, he stated his case succinctly and to the point.

Then he listened to his prospect tell him why he should have the extra coverage. Again, the right words at the right time aimed at the right target—thanks to sixth sense insight.

Of all the arts and skills a professional salesperson needs, the most important is listening with the inner ear of the sixth sense. This may sound a bit like "Cloud 9" stuff, but it's really quite real and dependable.

A professional salesperson must listen to the total message coming toward him or her as the sale is being made. Remember what my friend Red Motley said: "You never hear the sales talk that sells you." And that's what I have found to be the fascinating challenge of selling . . . helping a person build up reasons for buying, without feeling a sale is being made.

To accomplish this artful objective, complete and total "listening" must be attuned to the prospective customer. I have always felt that a message coming from the spoken word carries several levels of information.

First, there is the information coming from the words being spoken. In many cases, a customer cannot find the exact word to express true feeling. So, you must listen intently to what is trying to be stated with words but falls way short—such a person is telling you he or she needs more help to understand what you are presenting.

Second, there is information coming from what is *not* being said. Many times people want to say something, but feel it would present them in the wrong light, so they skirt around what they really feel. At this level, intense concentration and sixth sense insight is needed because there are so many shadings to be accurately interpreted. For instance, is the prospect trying to ask about price without seeming to be cheap? Or is he trying to hide the fact that making a decision is too hard to handle?

Third, the entire time you are selling, there is body language information coming toward you. Is the person nervous and jerky . . . or calm and collected? Does the person indicate with hand and arm movements that he or she is impulsive, or quite analytical? This information controls the direction of your sales presentation. The nervous and jerky type information tells you to interpret your sales story with emphasis on emotional dimensions, since this area will probably be the most productive in making the final buying decision. On the other hand, the calm and collected person is giving you an invitation to present facts and logical reasons for deciding to buy what you are selling.

As you strive to tune in on these three broad information levels, keep asking yourself where your prospect fits into the three basic psychological needs:

Identity: Does your prospect give you the feeling that he or she is self-oriented and well adjusted as a person? Or does your prospect give you the feeling he or she needs to be reinforced and made to feel secure in the buying decision?

If your prospect has a strong sense of self-identity, then it is much easier to relate to that identity with specific benefits from your product or service. If that identity is not strong, then you face the challenge of feeling just what image is important to your prospect and building on that psychic need or material want.

Stimulation: The psychic need for something *new* is most important. Some people realize this importance but many do not. Instead, they moan and groan about being bored in life. What they are really saying is, "Help me experience something new!"

If such is the case, then search your mind for the new features of your product or service and begin to relate to the imagination of your prospect by showing how enjoyable these *new* features will be.

It is amazing in our society to observe the magic of the word new! There is promise of excitement and pleasure in seeing and buying something new—a breakthrough, a completely *new* product.

When advertising copywriters reach for the magic buying words, they usually get the word *new* in the headline. This is why the giant soap companies are always coming out with a "new" product to chase dirt or control your hair—they know that if they tune out boredom, they'll tune in sales!

Security: The concept of security is different for just about every person. If you ask a friend what the word security means, the answer usually comes back in terms of material wealth in one form or other. Yet, some of the most mentally insecure people I have ever known had great material wealth. But they yearn for peace of mind, for that inner security that permits a calm outlook on life.

Offhand, I'd say the greatest inner security comes from being able to cope creatively with whatever comes along. If you get the sixth sense feeling that your prospect is lacking in a sense of inner security, then move at once to show how your product or service can give an inner feeling of well-being because of what it will do.

Relating to these three basic areas of identity, stimulation, and security is an art. First of all, it's important to sense through quiet listening just which of these three areas means the most to your potential customer. This requires the art of oblique approaches. Once the emotional target is clearly seen, then the soft sell begins. Let's take the selling of an automobile for an example of using this process of sixth sense selling, showing at what point the salesperson pulls back and lets the prospect do the selling. Our scene opens with a couple in their mid-thirties driving up in front of the automobile dealership's display window. As they walk in, the salesperson automatically begins qualifying the potential buyer.

He can tell they are here to buy a car by the way they walk to the door with confident steps. He can tell that they are the type of couple that manages the business of living on a planned basis. By the way each walks with confidence and pride, he assumes that they both work.

Fifteen years ago, you would assume that the man

would make the buying decision on a large purchase such as an automobile. Today, however, our salesperson is smart enough to know that times have changed. He does not make this assumption. As a matter of fact, he can't even assume that they are married! Let's listen in and see how this sale is made as the salesperson opens the conversation:

"Good morning," he says with an upbeat in his voice. "Thank you for coming to see our beautiful automobiles." (Not, "Can I help you?")

"Thank you," she replies graciously. "You certainly have some beautiful models this year. . . . We are particularly interested in a two-door sports model."

Tip Number One: It is the woman who responds.

By now our salesperson has observed a wide gold band on the lady's ring finger. He now assumes they are married. Since there was no diamond engagement ring, it seems logical they are the practical type who don't go for frills. He also notices the lady is wearing a tailored blue coatsuit. And the man is wearing white shirt, blue tie, and dark blue suit.

At this point, the man interjects: "What we need is a practical sports car that will give us good gas mileage. Have you got one like that? . . . We really don't need a four-barrel carburetor, you know."

Now the salesperson is summarizing in his mind very quickly. He has picked up tips two, three, four, and five.

Number Two: Practicality is a concern of both these prospects.

Number Three: Conservatism is important, as reflected by the blue suits they are wearing.

Number Four: Economy is more important than high-power performance.

Number Five: They both like the color blue.

It's important to realize all of the information our salesperson has picked up. Yet practically all the prospects have said is "Howdy" and "We want a sports car."

These five buying tips or cues are the obvious ones to a professional salesperson. It's the sixth sense cues that are now going to get the job done and the order signed.

First of all, it seems clear that our prospects are not to be swayed by emotion. They like to weigh things out and make sound decisions. Not much room for emotional selling.

They like to let it be known that they are in command of buying this automobile. Sound decisions will triumph, and the "Ms." will be leading the "Mr." in the decision process.

In addition, our salesperson picked up the wafting of a sexy perfume the "Ms." is wearing, which is a cue beyond apparent cues. This adds a new dimension to the buying incentives—and a complication. You see, the "Mr." is not very sexy—but his wife wishes he were.

Our salesperson also picks up a sweaty odor from the "Mr." as he passes by. Since he doesn't appear to be the athletic type, this speaks to the fact that the "Mr." is probably tense and nervous.

Now we have one key question regarding the blue suits both prospects are wearing. Which one is dressing to please the other? Since the woman is wearing the tailored suit, the feeling comes through that the man is dressing to please the woman.

To a professional salesperson, all of these cues are quickly picked up. The trick is *using* them all in selling the car.

How does it all come together so that the two prospects end up selling each other while the salesperson simply stands by and nods agreement?

First of all, this entire recitation of buying cues is

picked up in less time than it takes to talk about it. By the time the salesperson is walking these two prospects to see a car on display, he has a sales strategy worked out to fit them. As they walk toward the first car, he's thinking to himself, "I'm not going to show them the car I'm going to let them buy. I'm going to let them discover that car for themselves and then let them sell me on buying it. They are a sucker for blue, so I'll show them the tan car first. Then we'll stroll over by the blue job."

And so it went. The salesperson took them to the tan car and had both of them sit in it to get the "feel" of the car. It had the two-barrel carburetors, six cylinders to save gas.

The "Mr." began acting like he really appreciated this particular model. He didn't say so in words, but his body signals were saying "Yes!"

As they walked around the rear end of this tan job, the salesperson drifted over toward the blue car. As he did so, the "Ms." drifted with him and began to glance at this car with interest in her eyes.

"Now, this car has eight cylinders and four-barrel carburetors . . . I believe your husband wouldn't want this car. Of course, it has all the features of the tan car, plus extra power for passing on the highway. It's got an awful lot more for only a few hundred dollars' difference."

The salesperson could see that the "Ms." is now taking a serious interest in this blue job. So he figures now is the time to become silent and let "Ms." sell "Mr."

And so it happened. After about ten minutes of soft talk between these two on the far side of the car, the "Ms." walked over to the salesperson and said: "We like this one. Let's see what we can work out to buy it this afternoon." *Bingo!* the sale was made! Remember what Red Motley says: "You never hear the sales talk that sells you!"

Chapter Ten:
How to Get Accurate Impressions of a Person Over the Telephone

"You can develop an ability for telephonic telepathy."

Harold Sherman

To anyone unacquainted with extrasensory perception, it would seem impossible for any sensitive to tune in over the telephone on the mind of a person he may never have seen and get accurate impressions of what that party is like and how he really feels. Let me assure you, however, that there are psychically endowed men and women who are capable of sensing knowledge in this manner. And you yourself can learn how to do it if you so desire.

For some years now, I have been accepting telephone calls forwarded to me by my ESP office in Little Rock. Many people who have heard of me through my books or lectures are seeking help in locating missing planes and persons, in solving crimes of one kind and another, finding lost valuables, and solving intimate problems. The often desperate requests pretty well run the gamut of human experience. I have had to install a private, unlisted phone to protect me against calls coming from numerous time zones at all hours of the day and night. I return these calls when my mind can be free to give attention to them; otherwise I couldn't get any work of my own done. The callers obviously do not realize that they could be multiplied many times by others in trouble or distress. The urgency of their need blots out everything else.

I am often aided in the reception of thoughts by the fact that many who phone me are emotionally upset about something. Their intensity of feeling generates the power behind their thoughts, and as I listen to what they are saying, at the same time I am receiving impressions of what is really bothering them.

Sometimes it is not a personal experience, but something that has happened to a friend or loved one. If they are asking me for information that they have no knowledge of, I instruct my extra senses to reveal to me in imagery or feeling form what they wish to know.

Unbelievable as it may seem, my mind can often tune in on conditions and events concerning a missing plane or person or a murder, as though this knowledge is stored and on file in some "mental ether" or "dimension." I can see and feel it happening all over again, as I find words to describe it. I usually break in on the telephone voice and say: "Don't tell me any more. Let me tell you the impressions that are coming to me. I don't want to know any more details; they will only confuse me. Just listen—and when I am through, you tell me if what I am describing appears to be true or worth considering."

I am not always right. Many times the party calling has no way of knowing until a check is made of the impressions given, which might contain clues related to a murder, or where a missing plane may be found, or what may have gone wrong in flight, or where a body may be located. When I am tuned in on whatever the happening or experience, I often feel it so intensely that I get solar plexus reactions. When these feelings occur, it is usually the signal that I am on target.

Occasionally, although I seldom request it, I have been helped in the performance of psychometry, the psychic ability some sensitives possess for divining the history or events connected with a physical object with which a person has had close contact. This object could be a pair of shoes, pants, shirt, cap, knife, keyring—which somehow contains vibrations related to the individual's past or present activities.

One case, of many, best illustrates impressions that came to me by virtue of a telephone call, followed by my attempt through psychometry to enlarge upon the knowledge of what happened to a missing plane and its occupants.

It concerns a careful and exhaustive check of my

impressions by Don Winters, well-known West Coast physicist and close personal friend of the three prominent passengers, who had joined in a fruitless search for them after they had disappeared on a return flight from a fishing trip.

This account will demonstrate more than anything I could otherwise explain how these extrasensory powers function. His report of my ESP findings follows:

On Sunday, May 16, 1965, a single-engine float plane took off on a Seattle-bound flight from a small lake in north-central Washington. Aboard the plane were the pilot, Sidney Gerber, and two companions, Wing Luke and Kay LaDue, who were returning from a week-end fishing excursion at Lake Wannacut near the Canadian border. The westward route to Seattle lay across the rugged Cascade Mountains bisecting the state of Washington.

The weather situation on that day was highly uncertain, but at the time of departure from Lake Wannacut, the flight appeared feasible. In mountainous areas, however, flying conditions are often subject to change and can become treacherous in the extreme. On this occasion, the weather along the homeward route deteriorated not long after Gerber and his companions took off. A frontal system moved into the Cascades and developed into a storm of unusual ferocity, considering the time of year. After a brief radio communication over Lake Wenatchee, just to the east of the mountains, the plane disappeared completely, without a single clue as to the fate of those on board.

Tragic mishaps involving small planes are not infrequent occurrences in the Cascades, and this episode might have been given no more than modest publicity were it not that the persons involved were individuals of considerable prominence in the community. Sidney Gerber was a local businessman with a long-standing dedication to civil rights causes. He was the organizer and director of Seattle's Fair Housing Listing Service and former chairman of the State Board Against Discrimination. Wing Luke was a member of Seattle's city council, with a reputation for exceptional vigor and effectiveness, and Kay LaDue held a position as secretary with the Metropolitan Democratic Club of Seattle. The city could ill afford the loss of such progressive citizens, and on Monday, May 17, there was initiated the most intensive and expensive air search ever undertaken in the area. The search effort was supervised by William Gebinini, at that time director of the Washington State Aeronautics Board. The level of funding for air rescue allowed for an official search lasting ten days, during which time numerous aircraft inspected thousands of acres of wilderness without success. In addition, naval reconnaissance planes photographed thousands of square miles of mountain terrain. Despite the closest scrutiny, the pictures revealed no trace of the missing plane.

This discouraging turn of events was not altogether unexpected since the probability of sighting a small aircraft in mountainous or forested regions is rather low, even when its general location is known. In this particular instance, there were no helpful clues to localize the search area. I can personally testify to the enormity of the undertaking, since I was involved in the search effort. My motivation for participating was of a personal nature; Sidney Gerber, the pilot of the missing plane, was a friend of mine. In fact, another friend and myself had flown with Mr. Gerber over the same route to the same lake for fishing on the preceding weekend.

Sidney Gerber was a man of great vitality and courage, and it was difficult for many of us to accom-

modate to his loss. After a few days, it became clear that
since there was no clue to suggest a fruitful area, the official search was unlikely to succeed. One evening, as I
was pondering the situation, my wife reminded me that
she had an uncle in Arkansas who was involved profes-
sionally in research in extrasensory perception and that
he might be able to render some assistance. Being somewhat of a skeptic in such matters, I could not entertain
this suggestion seriously, but since nothing more was at
stake than the cost of a long-distance telephone call, I decided to go along with it.

Thus on May 26 we contacted Harold Sherman.
We gave him the names of the persons aboard the missing plane and began to describe the situation to him con-
cisely and without elaboration. In the midst of the conversation, after having mentioned the radio contact over
Lake Wenatchee, Mr. Sherman interrupted us and reported that a sequence of impressions was coming to
him. As he verbalized these impressions, I took notes in a
hasty fashion.

Sherman reported an immediate impression of the
plane being forced off to the right during a severe storm
and ultimately, of a crash that took the lives of all three
persons aboard. Although the impressions given during
the telephone call were interesting, we required information specific enough to identify a search area. Mr.
Sherman suggested that an attempt at "psychometry"
might yield further details if I could provide him with a
suitable object. It just so happened that I had in my possession a pair of shoes that Sid Gerber had given me and
that I had worn only on one occasion. I posted one of
these to Mr. Sherman at once and subsequently received
from him the following two communications, describing
psychometric impressions received on May 29:

"About forty miles beyond Lake Wenatchee, the

full force of the storm hits Gerber. I feel as though I am in the plane and being buffeted. It is carried to a higher altitude in an updraft and barreling off to the right, keeping a halfway forward motion against the force of the wind, hitting the left side of the plane.

"I feel we are being carried off course and the pilot is trying desperately to get out of this weather which has been steadily worsening. The velocity of the wind, with snow and hail now pelting the plane, makes it almost impossible to control it.

"Sid hopes to get above the storm, since it is dangerous to go down through it for an emergency landing . . . but the [storm] is too high. I know nothing about the geography of the country but sense its ruggedness and wildness. There are heavy timbered areas and mountain crags below and deep canyons not permitting a safe approach for a landing, especially in foul weather.

"Sid decides he must get down at all costs, since he cannot get out of the weather, nor can he turn back. The force of the wind makes the plane almost unmanageable, and I hear creaks and straining sounds and wonder if the plane is not even icing up. It begins to lose altitude, and the engine reacts to the hard going.

"Sid and his companions now recognize the desperateness of their plight and brace themselves for a possible rough landing. It seems that Sid has an area in mind—a body of water he hopes to reach—one he has landed on before. But he has lost visibility and a sense of direction. He realizes that he cannot call for aid— nothing can be done for him. Whatever can be done, *he* must do. . . .

"The plane is being carried far right from his intended course and Sid has great trouble keeping it on an even keel. He is now losing altitude fast, hoping he can get a ground view to level off for a crash landing.

"The plane narrowly skims a crag and treetops,

shoots across a canyon, and runs into an updraft, a swirling one from a deep ravine. It is blown like a kite and hits into trees and a mountainside about a quarter of a mile or more above what seems to be a river and a small waterfall.

"I feel Sid was killed outright, and as the plane cracks up, the other two may have been thrown clear, badly injured. . . . They are still in a bad storm area, and if the other two did temporarily survive, I feel it was not for long. I do not get a 'live' feeling as I put my mind on the three. I am sorry to have to report, for whatever these impressions may be worth, that I do not sense survival.

"I feel some weeks later—under ideal weather conditions—a pilot flying over the area may sight some spots of color from plane fragments, and perhaps a Forestry parachutist might be dropped—or a helicopter get down to within a quarter or half a mile of them."

Later, on June 15, 1965, Sherman tried again:

"Gerber a powerful man, fearless, sure of himself, almost reckless at times. . . .

"Same sensation. . . plane in storm, veering off to right. Gerber fighting to keep on course, gives up and has only one thought—to get down out of weather. He tries for a water area and a water landing, but I still feel he does not make it. . . .

"He is blown into side of mountain. . . trees, and I get sliding sensation as though fragments of plane drop into ravine. Difficult to detect from air. If I am right, about a quarter to half a mile from stream or lake, old logging road or camper's road to left of area where plane crashed. . . .

"Could be wrong, but still seem to be spots of snow nearby—strips of white. . . .

"A cabin or two, a mile or more ahead of place where plane down. No one seems to be there at present—wild. . .main highway possibly ten miles. . .and to right of location. . . .

"Looking down from air, I seem to see land sloping to left from higher elevation on right, where plane crashed. . . .

"I never get direction—north, south, east, or west —and never consult map or want to know layout of country. . .so mind will not invent or activate imagination. . . ."

Having these remarkable impressions in hand, we set about the task of gathering additional data, including specific details concerning the storm at midday and possible foul weather routes. The relevant information can be briefly summarized as follows. A weather front moved across the Cascades during midday on May 16. By noon, the front had become well defined and was situated in the vicinity of Stevens Pass, as reported by a group of mountain climbers to the south. The weather that preceded the front was characterized by a cloud cover at six thousand feet and by scattered snow showers. In the vicinity of the front, an ice storm of considerable intensity had stopped vehicular traffic on Route 2 over Stevens Pass at midday. The winds were predominantly NNE, gusting to 50 or 60 m.p.h. To the east of the Cascades (ahead of the front), the ridge crests were obscured by clouds although the valleys were still clear. Snow showers were developing in that area, as well.

Under the circumstances, it seemed to us unlikely that a small plane could have survived an attempt to fly through Stevens Pass. Yet Harold Sherman's impressions of May 29 began with the statement "about forty miles beyond Lake Wenatchee. . . . " We were told that when westbound pilots report their position to Wenatchee as "over Lake Wenatchee," they are often situated several miles to the east of the lake. Measuring distance from such a point, it was conceivable that the pilot first flew toward the pass, then altered course to negotiate the pass by way of the Rainy Creek drainage and failed in this attempt.

The Rainy Creek area has many of the features set forth in Sherman's May 29 impressions, but the impression of "forty miles beyond" would need to be interpreted with considerable freedom. On the other hand, we decided to rule out the possibility of a flight directly through Stevens Pass on account of the weather situation prevailing at that time.

We searched some likely areas of the Rainy Creek drainage without success. The chances of survival were now becoming extremely remote, and the time finally came when we decided against making further attempts to find the missing plane. When the summer drew to a close, I became convinced that the plane would never be located.

A few months later we received a greeting card from the Shermans. In a postscript to this note we were informed that Harold Sherman had a strong feeling that the plane would soon be found. My reaction was that he was simply indulging in wishful thinking and I gave the matter no further thought.

A few weeks later, however, to my very great amazement I learned that Harold Sherman was right. On Thursday, October 3, 1965, a helicopter pilot on a geological survey flight spotted the wreckage of the plane in a mountainous region near the small town of Index in the Cascades. Excerpts from a newspaper report of the finding appear below (*Seattle Times*, October 6, 1965):

The plane which disappeared May 16, 1965, with City

Councilman Wing Luke and two others aboard has been found beneath a waterfall on Merchant Mountain six miles east of Index, Snohomish County.

Ron Pretti, director of the State Aeronautics Commission, said the wreckage of the Cessna 180 float-plane was discovered at 3 P.M. Thursday. A pilot for Aerocopters, Inc., was making a geological survey flight when he saw the wreckage.

He said it would have been extremely difficult for anyone to have sighted the wrecked white airplane because of the rugged terrain, snow in the area, the waterfall, and foliage.

"The plane was resting in a log jam on a rocky ledge and part of it was in the waterfall," he said. Engine cylinders were scattered about the crash scene, he said, and a wing tip, part of an elevator and other pieces were found about 200 feet away.

He said the area at the site consisted of jagged 75- to 90-degree slopes.

A reconstruction of the probable route of the plane was reported a few days later. Harold Sherman's initial impression that the terminal events of the ill-fated flight occurred "about forty miles beyond Lake Wenatchee" were correct.

Further correspondences emerge between Mr. Sherman's impressions and the probable course of events when consideration is given to the probable flight path and the weather. For example, the wind direction was such as to buffet the plane from the left over much of the route, and severe icing conditions existed in the vicinity where the plane was found. Furthermore, Sherman referred to a body of water where an emergency landing might be attempted. This could possibly be the Tolt reservoir, a few miles beyond the site of the crash. Both sets of impressions suggest the plane crashed into a mountainside where the slope was so steep that "fragments of the plane drop" from the site of impact. Reference to the newspaper account with photographs establish that this was correct.

In summary, it is fair to say that there exists a good

correspondence between Harold Sherman's impressions and the facts that are now accessible to us, together with inferences and reconstructions from these facts.

This well-documented case should dispel any doubts as to a sensitized mind's ability to gain specific information at a distance, either from other minds of persons, known or unknown, or from so-called higher sources.

I am assuming that few of you reading these lines would be interested in devoting the time and effort to develop your ESP powers to this degree. But I am reasonably sure you would often like to be able to intuitively read the thoughts and feelings of those you meet either in person or over the telephone.

A tone of voice tells you much, of course, but one's feelings can be masked. A pleasing voice can be very persuasive when the party is trying to sell you something, whether you think you want to be sold or not.

Because of the demands on me, I have listened to literally thousands of voices and I have gotten so that I can get an accurate picture of the appearance and nature of most men and women after a moment or two's conversation.

This is done by getting yourself out of the way. If someone is calling you, after a connection is made, divide your mind's attention on what is being said and what feelings are really behind the words. You will discover that often words and feelings do not jibe, do not go together. If this happens, be diplomatic. But go slow on too quick an involvement with the individual.

When you yourself are on the selling end of the phone call, watch your own words and feelings. Don't make yourself put in an important phone call when you are nerve-tired, not in the mood to expend your energy on contact with another mind.

Always remember that no conversation is just word-for-word, it is always mind-to-mind. Even without a person consciously being aware of how the other person is feeling, his extrasensory faculties are picking up things, so that an individual may say, "I don't know why —but I just can't buy what he's telling me."

If you do not start a phone conversation by a preconceived idea or memorized version of what you intend to say, you can better sense the trend of thought and feelings in the other party and adapt yourself to his or her needs, interests, or desires.

You will know when to bear down and when to let up in any sales approach. Try keeping your inner mind passive when talking to others. On a personal call, you will often sense how a friend is feeling or what is troubling him without his mentioning it, no matter how he might try to cover up. "I wasn't going to say anything about it," he will sometimes remark when your comment or query has detected the real state of mind.

Keep a little record of your observations and reflections, and you will be surprised at how accurate your impressions are—and how helpful they can be in understanding everyone, seen or unseen.

Chapter Eleven: How to Conduct a "Mental Interview" With a Person *Before* the Actual Meeting

"Living ahead of the 'time frame' permits you to experience others' reactions to your organized presentation of positive picture images."

Al Pollard

Keen awareness and acute sensitivity to people are two important keys to the "mental interview." Equally important, of course, is the ability to project your mind and feelings into the reality of the other person.

This mental projecting requires a bit of the sixth sense.

Before this projecting begins, however, it's important to do some homework about the person to be interviewed. The first clear-cut goal to attain mentally is exactly what you wish to accomplish. In other words, what is the purpose of this interview? To what degree do you wish to influence the thinking of the other person?

Are you trying to sell a product, a service, or a point of view?

Are you trying to inspire the other person toward a new way of living?

Are you having to scold or chastise the other person? If so, do you have an approach that will leave a positive feeling?

Are you trying to get material for a biographical story?

Once you have a sharp image of what you wish to accomplish, then comes taking the mental inventory of the other person. This calls for knowing the other person, one way or another.

Personal experience with feeling is best. But information is information—if it is accurate. The important thing is to know all you can about the person you are going to sell, inspire, scold, or write about.

Self-Interest Is the Base to Build On

There is nothing more powerful in the world of human emotions than self-interest, the beginning and the end of all human relations.

If you develop the art and skill of always relating to the other person's self-interest, you will enjoy every hour of the day and night—both at work and at home.

Very few people understand this basic fact of life. Yet it is the secret to "people relations" at whatever level of life you wish to select.

For this reason, it is imperative that you have an accurate feeling for the other person's self-interest when you conduct your "mental interview" before the actual meeting. Without this knowledge, you will be missing many opportunities to "turn on" your subject.

In developing thoughts that relate to the other person's interest, it's important to assign priority to the ideas that will mean the most in your one-on-one discussion. This, of course, assumes you have done your homework and you know which ideas will mean the most. In other words, don't conduct your "mental interview" on a willy-nilly basis. Structure what you are going to say based upon thought impact to the *other* person. This calls for a clear mental image of what comes first, second, third, and so on. You must have a beginning, a middle, and a close. And the transitions must be so smooth that the other person is not aware you are changing the subject.

Questions Should Relate to Psychic Needs and Material Wants

Experience shows that questions that do not threaten stir up conversation in a positive vein, rather than in a defensive or aggressive vein.

One of the best questions in this approach is the one that starts out like this: "Mr. Smith, what would you think of a situation that would do the following. . .?"

This approach does not challenge Mr. Smith. You have given him an open-ended question that gives him a chance to respond in accordance with his experience —rather than trying to justify a specific action he may have taken. In other words, you are not asking him to get on the record with an answer. This open-end approach is a smooth questioning technique.

So, as you begin to write out the questions you intend to ask, this is where your sixth sense swings into action. Since you have done your homework for the interview, you can now begin to call upon your subconscious mind for the answer your subject will probably be giving you.

As you sit quietly at your desk at home or in your comfortable reading chair, let your inner mind speak to you. In fact, let your inner mind (unconscious mind) play the role of your person to be interviewed. Call on your inner mind for the answer to the question you have posed. Keep your own outer mind's quick answer out of your inner mind. Your conscious or outer mind will quickly come up with an answer, but that's not the one you want. You are listening to your inner mind. Get mentally quiet . . . listen in the silence.

To do this, I have always thought in terms of shifting my conscious or outer mind into neutral gear. In other words, it stops thinking. It stops shooting ideas at you based upon analysis of fact or experience.

This mental quietness permits ideas and feelings from your unconscious or inner mind to pop into your consciousness. In other words, you don't let your logical outer mind challenge ideas popping through from your inner or unconscious mind, which is your creative mind.

People ask me: "How can you tell if you are getting an idea from your unconscious mind? How do you know if it isn't your conscious mind giving you the message?"

The best answer I can give is that these "popping" ideas feel right! . . . You don't have to stop and ask yourself: "What is wrong with this idea?"

You have a strong inner sense of "being right." These are what some people refer to as strong "gut level" decisions. These decisions are made by leaders who make it clear "the buck stops here."

So, in preparing yourself for an interview with Mr. Smith, a man whom you know very well, you assume in your quietness that you *are* Mr. Smith. You begin to consider whatever it is you wish to achieve, in the light of Mr. Smith's self-interest. At this feeling level, you begin trying to pick up his vibrations of interest. There is one thing to remember: Do not push for this kind of a feeling. Completely relax yourself. Let your conscious mind become dormant. Then, speak to your unconscious mind, much as you would to a friend sitting there by you. Say something like, "I want you to give me the feeling of how Mr. Smith will feel about this idea I am trying to present to him. I want you to pick up his feeling on this matter."

And then relax as deeply as you can. Just let go, and listen to the silence. Something may come quickly. But more than likely, it will not. So just continue to think about what it is you want to know. If you drop off to sleep, fine. Sometimes, it is in the gray area of consciousness that ideas begin to flow.

If you do nap and wake up with a strong feeling about Mr. Smith, jot it down so it doesn't get away from you. Write just as long as you feel compelled to do, then relax again. If nothing begins to flow, relax some more. Repeat the process for as long a time as you have to spare.

Assuming you do not get a feeling about Mr. Smith, get a blank pad and jot down ideas about Mr. Smith that you know from personal experience if possible. Draw a line down the middle of the blank page. At the top of the left panel write in bold letters the word PRO. On the opposite side of the page write the word CON.

Then try to continue getting a feeling as to how Mr. Smith may react to your presentation. The mere fact that you are concentrating on what you feel about him will help to get your deeper consciousness working on more answers for you.

At this point in the process of living ahead of the time frame, it is time to check what feelings you have picked up against what you perceive to be Mr. Smith's psychic needs and his material wants.

Through "listening in the silence" you may have picked up some feelings about the psychological needs of Mr. Smith—hopefully so! Because it is this level that is most important since it controls the ego expression and sets the pattern for material wants.

Once you have settled in your own mind on the deep-seated psychic needs, then your next strategy is to search your life's experiences as to what you have to share, to reinforce Mr. Smith's psychic needs. This is most important because it permits you to open your interview up with a mental gift to Mr. Smith. Immediately, you can feel a rapport begin to build between the two of you.

Why? Because you followed the universal law: "First you give. Then you receive."

For example, let's assume that Mr. Smith has a deep-seated psychic need to be appreciated. He feels others take his efforts for granted. They do not understand how much he has done on any given project. In short, he is starved for attention and appreciation.

You have picked up this feeling of his psychic need in your former experiences with him. In your silence, it comes to you loud and strong that this psychic need holds the key to having a successful meeting with him. So what do you do?

First of all, you must be completely sincere in whatever you do. Without this sincerity, you are simply conning Mr. Smith—and the world doesn't need any more con artists.

Your opening remark might be something like, "Mr. Smith, I've always felt that you have a unique talent for the position you hold. Have you ever thought of yourself as being an outstanding specialist?"

"Well, you might say that," Mr. Smith replies with humble pride. "I have spent many years learning all I know about this business. I guess you might say I am a specialist, but nobody around here ever thinks of me as such. Guess I have been here too long."

Words like these open the door to a heart-warming interview. Mr. Smith has responded to your first observation: he has shown that he doesn't feel appreciated. Your intuitive feeling about Mr. Smith is right on target. Now, what's next?

With this kind of response from Mr. Smith, the first thing to do is to speak to his being an expert with *specific* ideas. Let him expand upon what he feels and thinks. This conversation should be carried on just as long as Mr. Smith warms up to the subject. There is, however, a point at which Mr. Smith will come to a natural slowdown on the subject of himself and how he isn't appreciated.

At that point, you shift from the psychic need to his material wants. This is where you show your own sensitivity in being able to make a smooth transition from need to wants.

Let's assume the purpose of your interview is to sell Mr. Smith on taking the general chairmanship of the United Fund Drive in his town. Everyone has agreed he would be terrific if he would take the job. But everyone also knows how big a load he carries in his business. It is doubtful if he will even give a second thought to accepting this civic responsibility. So the immediate challenge is to make a smooth feeling transition from talking about appreciation of his expertise into the subject of the interview.

"You know, Mr. Smith, I don't believe you know how many people in this community really appreciate all you've done to help create new jobs and better payrolls. You are well liked and respected across the entire city."

At this statement, Mr. Smith raises an eyebrow as if questioning the sincerity of your statement, but deep down he seems to appreciate what you said. In other words, he *wants* to believe—but he's not quite sure.

At this point you must become extremely aware and sensitive to what is being said, what *isn't* being said, and what is *desired* to be said. This is the critical point in the interview when you again call on your sixth sense to guide you through this key point in your transition to your true objective. Your next statement should be along this line:

"You know, Mr. Smith, this community owes you its top honor to really show you deep appreciation for your service. We really ought to award you a large plaque to hang on your wall for everyone to see." (The plaque is a subtle transition in satisfying Mr. Smith's deep desire for material things that will reflect appreciation.)

"Whatever I've done to help has been my pleasure," Mr. Smith says with genuine simplicity.

At this point you begin feeling that now is the time to begin moving into the heart of your interview. So you begin picturizing in your mind the strong image of Mr. Smith saying the words you want to hear, such as, "Well, I *am* very busy, but I guess it's my turn to take out enough time to help our community."

If these are the simple words you want to hear, continue to burn these words into your conscious mind. And you concentrate on projecting them into the mind of Mr. Smith. The point to be remembered is that this is the way you lived the interview in your mind's eye before the actual meeting. You are now doing what you picturized in advance of the actual face-to-face interview. It's now time to go for the commitment you want. Listen to yourself as you say:

"Mr. Smith, this community needs you much more than you realize. You have a real talent for getting people to work together."

At this point, Mr. Smith is beginning to smell a rat. By the direction of this last remark, he can tell that he is being set up for something; he doesn't know just what. So he listens. You get the feeling that his defenses are going up, so you come to the point: "The fact is, Mr. Smith, our community needs you this fall. We need you to pull together our United Fund organization. It's been drifting the last five years. As you may recall, we fell short of our goal this past year. This simply means our people in this community are not motivated to get out and get the job done. Those of us concerned about this failure know you are the only one who can get it back on track."

During this statement, Mr. Smith is idly tapping his pencil on his clean desk. You can see that his disciplined mind is walking around the challenge you have just given him.

Whether or not Mr. Smith will accept this civic responsibility will depend upon how skillfully you continue to feed his psychic needs and material wants. The scene is all set properly because you have lived this experience ahead of the time frame of actual occurrence. You did your homework. You spent the time to get the feel of your prospect's needs and wants. And then you appealed to them in a supporting manner—with *complete sincerity.* In short, you were taking all the steps necessary to actually experience the interview before it took place.

You harnessed your sixth sense in a way that can enrich every personal experience you may have—because you have discovered how to become keenly aware of those around you, at all times. Your sensitivity to people has been increased beyond your fondest expectation!

Chapter Twelve:
How to Control the Thinking of a Group Through ESP

"Anticipating the common denominator of feeling in a group is the first step toward tuning in the actions and reactions reflecting individual needs and wants to be nourished."

Al Pollard

Americans attend more meetings than any other people in the world. It seems every time you turn around, there is another meeting to attend for one reason or another.

Businessmen in Europe find it hard to understand why American businessmen give away so many of their trade secrets to one another. . . . Why are we always sharing what we have learned?

Europeans are quite secretive in their business relations. They are not interested in sharing ideas and experiences that have cost them much money to achieve.

Perhaps in America we are still relating to the pioneering experience of helping each other build a country, a home, a barn—or a family relationship.

Whatever the reason, one fact stands out in bold relief. Not one American in 100,000 knows how to run a meeting so that it is productive in the shortest period of time. I feel this is true because very few chairpersons are even aware of the intuitive process as it applies to successful meetings.

For instance, how many chairpersons do you know who are even aware that ESP or intuitive feelings hold the key to a successful meeting?

Do you think that they have seriously considered the concept that when you are striving for agreement on a plan of action, feelings come before facts?

From a practical standpoint, I have seen more meetings hung up getting nowhere for the simple reason the chairperson was concerned with "who's" right and not "what's" right. This is why I am firmly convinced feelings are the basis for serious consideration in every meeting.

Through years of sitting in meetings and conducting meetings I have evolved a checklist that comes in handy when I'm putting together an agenda for action. The ten items on this checklist are all aimed at the feeling level of participation.

This list serves as a reminder course, much the same way as commercial airline pilots have to check their "op sheets" before each takeoff. It is so easy to get caught up in facts and forget feelings when you are dealing with a group of people.

Meeting Management by ESP

As you have read in the preceding chapter, it is possible to have a mental interview with a person before you ever meet personally. This same process applies to pulling a meeting together so it will fly.

Mentally meeting with one person in advance of the interview is one thing, but living ahead of the time frame for a working meeting involves multiple personalities. Each person at the table has his or her own ego to satisfy. In addition, if you are the chairperson, you have certain objectives that must be reached if the meeting is to be productive.

So this is why I have evolved through the years a checklist of objectives against which I measure the different personalities involved. These ten areas contain successful elements of any meeting. They are what I consider the Classic Meeting Goals:

1. Stimulate discussion.
2. Encourage listening.
3. Balance discussion.
4. Avoid aggression.
5. Break up controversy.
6. Keep the meeting alive.
7. Get through the agenda.
8. Reach conclusions.
9. Initiate positive action.
10. Create enthusiasm for follow-through.

Behind each and every one of these ten areas for Meeting Management lie the personal feelings of everyone one sitting at the table. The challenge is to be aware of these feelings prior to getting down to business. In other words, you should have an in-depth understanding of each personality you will be working with throughout the agenda. If you haven't had the privilege of meeting the participants prior to the meeting, you have to "shoot from the psychic hip" as you go along. It is important you "rev yourself up" to a high degree of sensitivity, observation, and concentration. You must feel every word that is said, every accent given for emphasis, and every expression projected during discussion. And we haven't even mentioned watching all the body language—especially the women with the high-split skirts!

The process for meeting an individual involves relaxed moments for getting the feel, but the shoot-from-the-psychic-hip approach is just the opposite. You get so sensitive to the people at the table that a person walking into the room upsets receiving thought vibrations. Sometimes, if a door slams loudly, you will actually flinch.

I have always found that if you are really concerned about the outcome, the important minutes are just before a meeting starts. So it is my style to greet individuals as they come in with some kind of a supportive remark that will turn them on. Rather than just: "Howdy, how are you? Glad to see you."

What's the point? To get people relaxed and talking with one another. It's most important to break the conversational ice prior to the meeting and set the tone for the "sit down" session.

As a matter of fact, the sitting down *itself* is important! Where people sit is a message in itself. Some don't want to face the glare. Others don't want to sit too close to the seat of authority. Others just want to sit at the end of the table so they can slip out without being too conspicuous.

Then there are those who want to sit under your nose, so they can be in on all the action. Usually, they like to talk too much. Because of these experiences, I always prefer meeting at a round table—no authority seat and more neighborly to create participation. If a round table isn't available, I usually arrange tables so they form a square. This has almost the same effect as a round table.

As for the room itself, try to have plenty of space so participants don't feel their turf is being stepped on. But don't have people sitting so far apart that they feel like individuals rather than members of a group.

Temperature? Keep it cool. Nothing is worse than a hot, stuffy room that's too small for physical comfort. This destroys ideas quicker than a fat buzzing fly and perspiration dripping off your forehead.

How to Stimulate Discussion

Every meeting has its own personality. It is the composite of all those participating. Thus, some meetings are productive because the participants are disciplined to think in a straight line. Others are noisy and rambling for the opposite reason. There is no disciplined thought. Ideas bounce around the wall like a rubber ball.

In between these two extremes, most meetings occur. The challenge is always: "How can I, the chairperson, bring out the basic wisdom in this group of people? What can I do or say? How can I arrive at a working consensus? How do I stimulate productive discussion? How do I get to the feeling level of these people?"

I have always found it helpful to open the meeting with statements that can get everyone's head nodding "yes." Whether or not they actually nod their heads is unimportant, for you are *sensing* reactions to your statements. You feel these reactions . . . you equate what you are seeing and hearing and feeling from each person with your "pregame plan."

These opening statements should give an overview of what you propose to accomplish by the end of the meeting. These remarks may seem to be offhand, but they are not. The more spontaneous they may seem, the better. Since you have lived ahead of the time frame, *picturizing* reactions to your trigger words, you can expect your introductory ideas to lay the seedbed for productive discussion.

The trick now is to stimulate discussion in the direction you want it to go. At this point, begin recalling which person at the table seems the most receptive to your broad brush statement. Since you are operating from an agenda, everyone knows which subject area to discuss. So it comes as no surprise when you open the discussion with a question regarding item number one on the agenda.

After a brief introductory statement by you to set the feeling for this subject, you turn to your "friend" at the table and ask an open-ended question that does not require an immediate position. Rather, you are fishing for a general statement regarding the subject. This statement then opens up the subject. Others listen. You watch very carefully for reactions. You try to feel these reactions as they come toward you from each person at the table.

The key is your opening question, which must be open-ended enough to allow freedom of reply without need for defense of any kind. If this reply is so "neuter" that it does not spark a reaction from another member at the table, then you must move toward your next "friend" at the table and relate to what had just been said. But then end your remark with a more pointed question.

All the time this is going on, you must be taking the mental pulse of each member at the table. This is done so casually that no one is aware you are weighing them in the scale of conversation.

As the meeting gets under way, you are checking all the time with your "meeting-ahead-of-the-time-frame" which you *picturized*. It is important to see if your appeals to self-interest are working as anticipated. In your mind you are running a checklist of those who are responding as anticipated. If some are not responding as you picturized, then *you* need to take the verbal initiative—in saying things specifically aimed at those needing encouragement to speak.

Once you get under way and the meeting begins to gain momentum, it then becomes necessary for you to watch that people don't get so intent in what they are saying that they fail to hear what others are saying.

How to Encourage Listening

When participants all begin talking at once, a chairperson sometimes has to act as a referee. Frequently, an issue that's charged with emotion gets out of hand. Everyone wants to get in the act! Obviously, no one is hearing what the others are saying. But you are listening to everyone talking with great feeling. You are making a mental note of their boiling point.

Since you cannot ignore such a heated reaction, you are listening for key points that have the most bearing on the subject under discussion. After you have pinpointed the most significant thing said, you call for order and get everyone quiet.

First, you congratulate everyone on having said so much so fast! This gets a bit of laugh to ease the tension. Then you say something like: "In listening to all of you the best I could, I heard Mr. Brown make a statement I wish he would repeat."

So Mr. Brown is somewhat flattered that you called on him. The others at the table are wondering what he said that was so much better than what they had to say.

While Mr. Brown is talking, you are casually watching others at the table to see who is really listening. Some will probably be doodling on the agenda and others looking off into space.

Of those listening, you select the one who seems to be in accord with what Mr. Brown is saying. Then you summarize in your own mind the meat in the coconut of what has just been said. With that thought in mind, you pose a direct specific question to the person most receptive. In short, you ask for reaction to the basic idea. In this way, you are getting control of the thought content by screening out splattering ideas that do not help the meeting achieve a consensus.

Following this type of give-and-take, you may feel it is time for some sharper listening. So you say something like this: "Folks, I would like to summarize what we have been discussing. Listen closely and let me know if I am accurate in reflecting how you feel about this issue."

This type of statement is most effective if you have been successful in balancing discussion pro and con.

How to Balance Discussion

One of the real challenges in balancing discussion in a meeting is to see that no one person dominates the discussion. It's easy to do, especially if you have a participant who loves to hear himself or herself talk. It happens all the time.

I have found a simple way to keep control of the meeting so that everyone has a say—pro and con. As you might expect, the more aggressive people will speak first. This is fine, because it opens the issue for discussion.

As such a person begins to speak, I make it quite obvious that I am making notes of the key ideas being presented. When this first person is talked out, I simply say: "Let me see if I have the key points you made." Then I read off what I have written. If I have touched on all his or her key points, then quiet reigns. At this point, I take the initiative and call on a person who I feel has a different view, saying something like:

"Mrs. Jones, you have heard Mr. Brown's key points. I am wondering if you have some others you would like to add?" I could see she was unhappy about what she was hearing. So my question opened the door for her to have a say without appearing to be defensive. This is most important for a pro and con discussion.

As Mrs. Jones begins making her key points, I am writing like mad to let her see that her views are being recorded. When she comes to a stopping point, I read back to her what I feel is important to her and to the issue under discussion. This approach gives the chairperson control of what is being said. More important, it organizes the listening so that the group can make good decisions.

How to Avoid Aggression

Much is being said these days about aggression versus assertion. Aggression is being looked upon as negative, whereas assertion is being presented as positive.

Whatever the fine point of difference, the fact remains that either style can be decisive in a give-and-take at a conference table. At a meeting in which a productive point of view is the goal, the trick is to minimize *both* aggressive and assertive talk.

So how do you do it?

As we said in the beginning, you have lived this meeting before it actually took place. You have *visualized* how you can appeal to the self-interest of every person at the table. In doing this, you have also made an evaluation as to which members will tend to be aggressive and assertive.

Therefore, you keep the initiative with these people. How? By anticipating their position and leading into it, rather than waiting for them to spring it on the meeting. For instance, you, the chairperson know that Mrs. Smith is dead set against cutting any trees in the forest so we can all have a place to camp out—and you are trying to achieve a consensus in favor of clear-cutting and replanting. Therefore, a question like the following can help dilute some of the aggression:

"Mrs. Smith, what do you feel is the weakest point in the argument for clear-cutting forests and replanting?"

What have you accomplished with such a question?

First of all, by the tone of your question, you have alerted the group to the fact that Mrs. Smith is *against* clear-cutting. Second, you have asked her to make a positive statement as to what is wrong with clear-cutting, without stating the issue that bluntly. So Mrs. Smith is in the position of making a positive statement instead of blurting out a negative indictment and making a five-minute speech on conservation. In other words, this question narrows the arena of discussion and permits Mrs. Smith to show how much she knows—or does *not* know —about modern forestry.

As she talks, you are getting the emotional reactions from participants around the table. You can get the feeling as to whether Mrs. Smith is making points or losing position in her argument. While she is talking, you are also making quick notes and checking the feelings around the table.

The point of this type of approach is that you dig into specifics instead of wasting time with speech-making on an issue reflecting only an emotional viewpoint. This approach is helpful in skirting controversy that seldom helps create a productive meeting.

How to Break Up Controversy

In all the meetings I have directed or participated in, I have never seen anyone win a controversial argument.

Very few people will change their minds at a meeting. True, new facts and new conditions can create new consideration for an argument or a position. But do not expect spectacular victories through emotional arguments.

In my people-relations work through the years, I have run many public opinion polls. From the countless surveys we have made, a basic relationship stands out in bold relief:

In polling for political purposes, you must accurately evaluate what percentage of the public is for a candidate and what percentage is against the candidate.

Then you calculate how many people have not yet made up their minds. It is this *last* group that you try to swing to your candidate, because the odds are tremendous that you will not get committed voters to change their support. Roll into this the emotional intensity of those "for" and those "against" and you will get a feeling as to which group will actually go to the polls and vote for their convictions.

So it is in your meeting. You have those who are strongly for the issue and you have those who are strongly against. As you conduct the meeting, make yourself highly sensitive to picking out those who have not made up their minds. Concentrate on picking up their feelings about the issue. Observe their reaction to factual arguments versus emotional statements. This will give you a clue as to how they may vote—if you must go that far in arriving at a consensus.

If you are really trying to sell a particular viewpoint, concentrate on your point of view and keep projecting it into the minds of those around the table. The more intensely you can concentrate, the better your message will be received in this mind-to-mind delivery system.

If you can reduce your point of view to several short words, do so, and continue saying these words and projecting the thought behind them. If you pour your entire feelings behind this thought, you will transmit with more power into the minds of others around the table.

As you proceed in this projecting technique, keep a sharp eye and ear for controversy-in-the-making. I have noticed that once a controversy breaks out in the open, it is most destructive to the overall tone of the meeting. Sometimes you even have to adjourn the meeting, since the issue has become so polarized that very little productive thinking will occur.

But if you do see storm clouds gathering, begin to seek an opening in the conversation. Without emotion of any kind, insert a question to the talker that will get his mind off the track he is pursuing. That question should be related to the subject area, however, so it does not seem you are trying to switch the subject entirely.

How to Keep the Meeting Alive

As I mentioned previously, every meeting has its own personality. If people at the table are strangers, they are more reticent about speaking out. If everyone around the table knows each other, then there is no trouble keeping the meeting alive.

Observe how closely participants are sitting. Too close is not good, nor is too far apart. A comfortable distance creates the right balance of space for each person.

The first objective is to get the meeting off to a good start. If you are working with strangers, take the time to go around the table and let each person introduce himself or herself. As you hear details as to where they come from and what they do, break in with a warm, supportive remark that makes the person feel more comfortable.

After the meeting moves ahead, you will continue getting strong feelings and insights as to the interests of each person. As you catalog these areas of self-interest, you begin to understand how to appeal to each person. It has been my observation that meetings get "on center" for various reasons. Here are some that I have observed:

1. *Talked out*: When a subject has been discussed from A to Z, there comes a point where a lull is inevitable. You can *sense* this point before it actually occurs. Let your instincts guide you to change the subject into an area relating to almost everyone at the table. Discussion will come alive again.

2. *Subject boring*: There is no substitute for appealing to the self-interest of participants. If you have to lead a discussion where there are very few self-interest "hooks" to hang your discussion on, you must create some. Otherwise, conversation will come to a dead end.

3. *Dull leadership*: There is constant opportunity to brighten the discussion with fresh ideas and facts that are stimulating to participants. If you don't take the time and trouble to find these key points, then you will kill your meeting.

4. *Issue too hot*: There are times when participants

will clam up because they do not wish to commit themselves publicly. This is a tough one. You have to tippy-toe around the edge of a hot potato. The best way is to ask for observation as to what seem to be the points of greatest concern. Do *not* ask for a position at this point. Try to get people talking about the issue itself—without the overtone of personalities usually involved.

5. *Uncomfortable*: Usually you can tell if people are too cold or too hot. In either case, the quick answer is to change the temperature if possible. People begin thinking more about how they feel physically than what they feel mentally. Change the environment, and you will liven up your meeting. Participants also get uncomfortable sitting for too long a period of time. Have a coffee break or a stand-up break, and things will change in a hurry.

Here again, I must stress that you, the chairperson, are responsible for a uniform flow of your meeting from topic to topic on the agenda. In fact, this smooth flow has its beginning in the alignment of topics as you arrange them for discussion. Pay attention to anticipating the flow of discussion so that one topic flows into the next one in logical sequence.

Above all, be an *alert*, *aware*, and *sensitive* chairperson! There is nothing worse than a meeting whose leader is not even aware that it is going downhill.

Instead, *visualize* the kind of meeting you want to have and then *concentrate* on it becoming exactly as you want it to be. Project a positive image at every stage of your meeting, and you will make it happen!

How to Get Through the Agenda

As a chairperson, you have the responsibility of creating a workable agenda. This is where your ability to experience your meeting "ahead of the time frame" will give you a feeling for what can be accomplished in a given period of time. *Picturize* your meeting as if you are presiding and working your agenda of subjects to be covered.

With practice, you will be able to glance at an agenda someone hands you and determine whether it will stay on schedule. If you will permit your sixth sense to operate, you will know what can be accomplished in the normal timing of most meetings.

In moving through the agenda on time, you *must* rely on your sixth sense to help you judge the level of participants. Some want to jump right in the minute you open the meeting for discussion . . . they enjoy jumping in and out at every chance they get. They are the time-stealers, and you have to find a positive way to shut them up so others can be heard.

Usually they begin to feel the peer pressure at the table and they ease off. On the other hand, I have seen meetings where the discussion was so brief the meeting was over an hour ahead of time. Most folks feel that's a godsend!

As for keeping the working meeting on schedule, there's one cardinal rule: Don't let people make speeches! True, every item needs consideration, but not through rhetoric.

I have found a positive way around this type of problem. At the beginning of the meeting, I usually say something like this:

"We have a lot of experience sitting around this table today. And I know we all want to hear from each other on the various items on the agenda. Also, we have a rather heavy agenda today, so let's all participate by making comments as we go along. But let's keep them brief so we can get through."

That serves as a warning that the chairperson may use the prerogative of breaking in on speech-makers.

Here again is a chance to use mind-to-mind communication. When a participant is getting a bit long-winded, I keep sending him or her the same short mental message: "*Shut up!*" Each time I say it with more and more inner feeling. It's not a polite statement. But who cares? No one hears it but me—and, hopefully, the long-winded one.

I once presented a rather large meeting in a new metropolitan hotel. I had all the new-fangled gadgets for presenting a great meeting. The one that appealed to me most was a speaker control system.

Speakers were told in advance that when they saw the yellow light flash on at the lectern, they had five minutes left in their accorded time. When the red light came on, that meant their time was up. And when the red light began flashing—that meant get the hell off the platform!

We had some rare comments from the speakers on the platform at the meeting. But we stayed on schedule. And that's tough to do when you have "that-reminds-me-of-another-story" speakers who get carried away with audience appreciation.

How to Reach Conclusions

Several years ago, I had the pleasure of attending a Ford Foundation Seminar in Bigwin, Canada, just north of Toronto. There were about three hundred people attending from most of the states.

Our seminar emphasis was the study of group dynamics. Our study focus was on the "Ways of Mankind." They broke up into tables of twenty with a discussion leader for each table. We had the pleasure of having Dr. Edgar Dale of Ohio State University as our leader. His excellent sense of humor and his ability to keep us all track-ing was quite impressive.

At our table was a broad mixture of talent. There were several Ph.D.'s, several social workers, several gov-ernment people, and several of us profit-and-loss charac-ters. I had the pleasure of sitting next to the president of the Pennsylvania Bell Telephone System. There were also a couple of presidents of large insurance companies.

The point of my story is simple. It has to do with arriving at conclusions.

At the end of about four days of intensive dis-cussion on the "Ways of Mankind" in the interest of con-tinuing education, I felt a bit frustrated. It seems we had waltzed around many subjects without being able to get a handle on any one as to how we could help stimulate continuing education.

Finally, at the last meeting, I had the audacity to say to the leader, "Dr. Dale, I have enjoyed every mo-ment of our discussion with you leading us. May I ask what we have concluded as a result of our discussions?"

To my amazement, the Ph.D. sitting across the table from me burst out with an emotional response: "What makes you think we have to conclude anything?"

Needless to say, there was quite a bit of response to that question from us profit-and-loss characters. But I shall long remember how shocked *I* was at this response! Having been honed in the business jungle, I saw very lit-tle reason for spending three days talking, without com-ing to a point of focus to guide some specific action.

To conclude that story, I must add that about two years and $8,000,000 later, a final report was written stating that the mission had failed in accomplishing its goal of increasing adult education.

I was not surprised.

That lets you understand how I feel about meet-ings ending without workable conclusions. Frankly, what is the point of having a meeting if there isn't a target to be hit with the combined thought power of the group?

It has always been my custom in running a working meeting—not an auditorium gathering—to summarize at the end of each item on the agenda. While the discussion is fresh on everyone's mind, I call for a summation. It's best if you let a proponent at the table do the recapping instead of you, the chairperson. If this is not workable, take the bull by the horns and make your own summation—with approval from the group.

When the meeting is concluding, read out the conclusions that have been agreed upon. More important, underscore the action that is to be taken on each item and who is responsible to get it done!

How to Initiate Positive Action

The purpose of meetings should be to focus a group's mind power onto a subject for consideration, with the end result being positive action. That, in my opinion, makes a productive meeting.

Even meetings that are basically informative should come to a conclusion related to future action. Simply reciting research or talking all around a subject without an action plan is a luxury few can afford.

The only purpose of knowledge is to hitch it to progress to help the world become a better place to live. To let knowledge lay idle on the shelf of your mind is a terrible waste of talent, time, and energy. For this reason, it is my opinion that much thought should be given to initiating positive action at every meeting—no matter what it was called for!

Here again, the chairperson must demonstrate personal *insight*. He or she must have a feeling for which person or persons at the working table have the ability and *motivation* to get a job done. I have always noted that a person in a given field is more motivated to work on projects relating to his or her field.

To make such a decision for giving responsibility for action, the chairperson must have a gut feeling as to which person will get the job done.

And at the risk of being simplistic, I personally feel that the chairperson owes suggestions for action to the person who is tapped for action. These ideas should be presented in the form of key suggestions as to what results you would like to have accomplished. It's the committee-person's responsibility to get it done.

This should be done in front of the entire meeting so that all can participate in the objectives as they are developed. By letting all participants be "in on" the proposed action, the committeeperson feels peer pressure to get the job done.

People seem to perform best when they are challenged properly. The chairperson should let it be known that this particular committeeperson has the exact expertise to do an outstanding job. People enjoy performing at the image level given them, especially by their peers.

How to Create Enthusiasm for Follow-through

There are two or three basic things to do to generate enthusiasm for follow-through with a committeeperson.

First and most important, at the meeting table, agree upon a specific date that certain action must be accomplished. Let everyone at the table write down this date to impress upon all the importance of the team swinging together to get an overall job done.

Second, there is no substitute for follow-through by the chairperson. It has been my experience that most folks are pretty busy. They get so enmeshed in their own lives and things to be done that they often let their committeeperson work slide to the back burner. I know this is true because I am more guilty than most of doing this very thing!

Third, if the committeeperson is having some difficulty in getting his or her job done as you feel necessary, schedule a luncheon and crank up some enthusiasm for what the committeeperson has done at that point. Then focus in on some ideas you have that could be helpful.

Fourth, at the next meeting of the total group, let all at the table know how much you appreciate the fine job they are doing. Make specific reference to specific people.

Believe it or not, the most shocking lack of leadership in the corporate world comes from leaders not showing proper appreciation for a job well done! So brag about your committeepersons. Make them *feel* warm and appreciated!

Overall, remember two outstanding rules for getting work done through people or committeepersons. Let them "Feel in on all you do" and "Show them appreciation for a job well done!"

Chapter Thirteen:
How to Change Negative Attitudes Through ESP Sensing

"Negative attitudes can be neutralized with positive mental images that create a new sense of direction and enthusiasm leading to productive action."

Al Pollard

What makes you and me think negative thoughts?

Why do we get our mental exercise by jumping at the wrong conclusions?

Why are we defensive and show the world we are lacking in self-confidence?

There are a couple of words that give a quick answer to these questions. The words? Ignorance and laziness! Let's talk about ignorance first.

What are you ignorant of? What is it you don't know? How can you learn to eliminate negative thoughts and negative attitudes? How can you keep from jumping at the wrong conclusions? And most important, how do you develop self-confidence that shouts to the world: "I can cope! Try me!"?

Let's start with one simple idea: You do have the power to control what happens in your life! You are not at the mercy of circumstance. You have the power to create the circumstances you desire! You and you alone can do it. But you have to believe with all your heart and soul that you have this power. You cannot pussyfoot around on this basic point.

Once you accept this idea, the next step is to understand how you make these circumstances happen. And that's where the fun begins. If thinking positive doesn't become fun for you, then you've missed a basic step along the line.

As my colleague Harold Sherman writes in this book: "Feeling is the power behind thought!" And feeling is the one thing you and *only* you can control. Therefore, you can control your thought patterns, which in turn control what you do.

So right now, ask yourself, "What feelings do I have about controlling the circumstances in my life?" If you answer that you have the strong feeling you can really achieve this control, then we go on to the next step.

Ask yourself now: "What circumstances do I want to create for myself?" Right here, we begin to separate the men from the boys. Because this is where you test yourself as to how high you want to climb the ladder of life. It's your decision—no one can make it but you.

Probably the most practical approach to evaluating the circumstances you wish to create begins with an inward look to evaluate your God-given talents. Make no mistake about it. You have inherited talents from your ancestors. It is said that grandparents have a distinct impact on your inheritance, more so than your parents. Whether or not this is true, the question is, Do you know the *strength* of your inherited talents? Have you ever taken inventory of yourself to understand what you do best? Negative attitudes grow best in your self-ignorance.

Why Do We Have Negative Attitudes?

We are focusing on how your higher powers of mind can help you change your negative attitudes. So let's go back to the original question: What makes you and me have negative attitudes in the first place?

A quick answer to that question is that out of ignorance, we drifted into negative attitudes over a period of years. Why? Because when this process was occurring, no one took the trouble to tell us we were violating basic laws of the universe! We were permitting our conscious mind to send negative thoughts into our unconscious mind. This inner or unconscious mind then went to work to help achieve what it *thought* we wanted: namely, negative things to happen.

So we went into an inside mental spin.

When you were a kid in school, did you ever have conscious thoughts like this? "I can't compete with my schoolmates. They're too smart for me. I can't compete in athletics because I'm not big enough. I can't learn to dance, I'm too clumsy. I can't meet people, I'm too bashful. I can't go out with boys, I'm too tall." Do these sound familiar from your growing-up days?

If so, then you had a bulging case of negative attitudes. This is the type of thinking that can be changed with the right mental processes.

First of all, there are some basic adult attitudes you must meet head on and renounce once and for all. Here is the list you are going to blast with ESP sensitivity:

"I'm a loser. Nothing I ever do turns out right."
"I'm afraid to try new things. I might fail."
"I just don't have what it takes to be successful."
"I wish I had more enthusiasm for doing things."
"I can't ever get going. Something always stops me."
"I don't have enough education to be a winner."
"I don't have any friends. Everybody is against me."
"I don't have any special skills to do anything."
"I don't enjoy what I do. Every day is a bore."
"I wish I had a different kind of job."
"I'll never marry. No girl would have me."
"I'll never learn how to drive a car."
"I'll never be able to get ahead in life. I don't know how."
"I'm stuck with the job I'm in and I hate it."
"I'm no good as a lover. Men laugh at me."
"I'm a woman. I'll never get paid like a man."
"I have a physical handicap. What can I do?"
"I can't make enough money to live on, so why try?"
"I hate people. They're no damn good."

Is it natural to think this way? Does everyone have similar negative thoughts?

Negative attitudes are generated out of pictures of fear given by your conscious mind to your unconscious mind. In other words, your outer mind, the reasoning mind, programs your inner, creative mind, with preconceived ideas. Since your inner mind contains all the experiences in life you have ever had, there may be some unhappy childhood experiences still giving you defensive signals—which come out in the shape of negative attitudes.

In other words, "Don't get exposed, and you won't get hurt."

This basic thought is behind most negative attitudes in life—for both kids and adults. It seems like a safe way to handle the business of living. But it's a sorry philosophy for living the happy, productive, fulfilling life.

Enthusiasm Overcomes Negative Attitudes

It's almost a cliché to say: "To get enthusiastic, be enthusiastic!" But that's the truth of the matter. The trick is how do you break the egg to make the omelet? What do you do to get enthusiastic?

To answer that question, let me tell you about an old black preacher friend of mine back in the twenties. He was a powerful preacher who led many wayward sinners back to the path of righteousness. I can still see him standing tall behind his pulpit, delivering the words of the Lord with powerful enthusiasm. He could really get his congregation stirred up in no time at all.

He was a respected citizen in our community. He had as many white friends as black friends. Everyone loved the Reverend.

One day he and I were sitting under a shade tree talking about life in general. Since I have always been interested in what it takes to move people into action, I asked him a question.

"Reverend," I said, "what is your secret to having

such a successful church? How do you get your congregation so involved in your services?"

I shall never forget his reply. It has stayed with me over the years as a glowing answer.

"Mistah Al," he replied, "I don't have a secret, but I'll tell you this. I got a *Glory to share*! Praise the Lord!"

Over the years, I have thought of the Reverend's answer many times. And it always keeps coming back that if you are going to have a "Glory to share," you have to get caught up in some particular phase of living that grabs hold of you and never lets go.

In other words, if you don't have some central part of your life bigger than you are, you just can't get up enough steam to be enthusiastic.

And that's how you break the egg.

Here's How You Make the Omelet

The recipe for making a "Positive Attitude Omelet" is to accept the idea that your inner mind will work for you twenty four hours a day at whatever you will it to do.

If you truly believe that, then the next step is simple.

All you have to do is know exactly what you would like to accomplish in life—so you can drum that mental image into your unconscious mind until it pulsates with your intense desire to accomplish your objective.

Now we come to the use of your higher powers of mind. We get into your having the exact mental image of what it is you want to accomplish as a major goal in your life.

When I say an exact mental image, that is exactly what you must achieve. A fuzzy image is no good. If what you want is a material goal in three dimensions, draw a picture of what you want. If you can't draw, cut out pictures from magazines and paste them in a scrapbook. You must have a precise mental image of exactly what you want to achieve.

In one of his books, Harold Sherman tells a story about the famous TV star Liberace that illustrates this principle better than any story I have ever read or heard. Liberace was so driven in his early career to get to the top that he envisioned himself playing in the great Hollywood Bowl to a sold-out audience. He got so carried away with this concept that he actually rented the Hollywood Bowl for an entire evening. He had the lights come up just as if he were actually presenting a concert to a packed house. For two solid hours he gave his complete concert in the Hollywood Bowl—without a single person in the audience! Two years later, he did pack the Hollywood Bowl and gave that same two-hour concert! How can you top that for picturizing what you want to achieve?

The secret behind this story is simple. What your mind can conceive, you can accomplish. If you don't have all the particular skills needed at the moment, the burning picture in your mind's eye will continue inspiring you until you develop the necessary skills.

Having such a clear and dominant picture of what you wish to happen will actually begin to attract to you the things needed for your success. As you go through your day's work, you let others know what you are visualizing to achieve. Your enthusiasm in "sharing your glory" will rub off on your friends. First thing you know, things will begin coming toward you that directly relate to helping you achieve your picturized goal!

As Harold Sherman has said earlier in this book, "In the realm of mind, like always attracts like." This is a magnetic law of the mind you can depend on. That is why it is imperative for you to concentrate on programming your inner mind with mental images of you achieving whatever it is you want to achieve—however small or large!

Creating Positive Mental Attitudes

If you are really serious about creating positive attitudes in your life, let's go about it in an organized way.

Get a blank tablet or sheet of paper and draw a line down the middle of the page. At the top on the left column write the words: *My Negative Attitudes*. At the top of the right column write: *Positive Attitudes I Desire*.

This writing down is most important for two reasons.

First, it is your way to admit privately to your negative attitudes. Some folks find this hard to do because they aren't even *aware* of having any negative attitudes! Once you have written yours down, study them to see if you have overlooked any.

Second, this is your way to get your first lesson in picturizing your objective, namely by listing all the positive attitudes you wish to achieve. This is most important.

After you have filled both columns with your statements, take another sheet of paper and recap the positive attitudes you want to develop. List each one and draw a line under it. Then write under that listing all the ways you would like to project your positive attitudes. Think of the image you would like to reflect to your friends.

Give concentrated thought and energy to this writing, because it is to be your image road map for the type of person you really want to be.

Once you have done this homework, the next step is even more important. Now comes the job of reviewing all you have written down—the negative and the positive.

Out of this material it is necessary you evolve an over-riding goal—the big goal that you wish to accomplish.

Bear in mind the mental process to achieve your big goal also works the same way to achieve your smaller objectives that lead to your larger goal.

So find a handle to your mental goal. A handle you can repeat to yourself time after time as you go through the day and night. Whatever the terse statement of your goal becomes, you must constantly say it to yourself all hours you are awake. This is how you burn it into your subconscious.

Each time you repeat this goal to yourself, pic-turize yourself actually living with whatever the goal is that you have created. This is most important.

To give you a personal account of how this process works, let me tell you a story of how I moved up in the world by visualizing. My company was housed in an office where it had originated in 1915. This year was 1960. I was seated at my desk, doodling on a layout pad. A lady who had made a date to see me about my ESP work came in as scheduled. She sat down next to my desk and saw my doodlings.

"I didn't know you are an artist," she said quite warmly.

"I'm not," I replied. "I do have enough ability to visualize what I am trying to achieve."

"And what is that you are visualizing?" she asked with perked-up interest.

"Oh, I'm getting ready to move to another office building, and I am in the process of living in my new of-fices before we move into them. It saves a lot of time in getting things shaped up the way you want them without having to do a lot of moving around."

"What do you mean, living in your new office be-fore you move?" she asked.

"It's quite simple, really. I have laid out the floor plan quite accurately and have visualized each piece of furniture and how it will fit into the new space. Then I walk around in the office and see if it feels comfortable. I have sat in my own office many times, trying to get the feel of where my books and furniture should be. As a matter of fact, I have redesigned this office about ten times to get it where it feels comfortable now."

To my genuine surprise, she seemed to be awestruck. She didn't say a word. After a few seconds of silence, I asked her, "How do you like this approach to moving?"

"It's fantastic! I don't know how in the world you do it!"

The point of the story is that many people do not comprehend the simplicity of visualizing. It seems to be a strange art to some. In reality, it's quite simple. All you do is compose in your mind's eye a scene that you wish to achieve—or a goal in life. And then you work toward that mental image. Both your conscious and unconscious minds work for you to convert your mental image into reality.

Once you have worked with this concept of creating the positive attitudes you want in life, you will be amazed at how easily this process becomes a way of life.

You become more aware! You become more alert! You become a fulfilled person!

What more can you ask of your conscious and unconscious minds?

Chapter Fourteen: How to Get Answers to Business and Personal Problems in Dreams

"Your subconscious can be instructed to solve problems for you in your sleep."

Harold Sherman

Your subconscious mind is a tremendous reservoir of creative activity. It is at work constantly, assembling and filing away for future use all the experiences and thoughts you have had during your *waking* hours.

No idea or feeling is ever lost, even though you may never be able to recall many of the impressions received from the conscious mind and stored in memory. But you will be influenced by the essence of everything that has happened to you, and perhaps without your realizing it, your emotional reaction to every event, big or little, is molding your character as well as changing your personality, for the better or worse.

It is well to remember that nothing can come out of your mind that you have not first put into it. This is another way of saying that *you* have the power to create pretty much what you want to do or be or have. This means you can go up or down, depending on the nature of your thought.

Which leads to the first question: What kinds of thoughts are you planting in your mind each night, upon retiring? Are you going to bed with a troubled consciousness, worrying over any unsolved or perplexing business or personal problems? If you are, like attracts like—and you are apt to awaken in the morning in a more unsettled state than before.

Actually, most of us are only using a small percentage of our mind's potential. Thomas Edison, America's great inventive genius, often repeated his conviction that man is only using one tenth of one percent of his brain power. Edison had discovered how to put the creative power of his subconscious to work for him. You've heard how he kept a cot in his laboratory. When he was struggling with an inventive problem, he would turn over all the information his conscious mind could gather to the subconscious part of his mind and instruct it to produce the ideas necessary for a solution.

Then he would stretch out on the cot and go to sleep for ten to fifteen minutes, confident he would awaken with the idea he was seeking. Time and again, his obedient subconscious servant, "Mr. Subby," would produce for him what he wanted or needed. If not, Edison would do some more visualizing and send some more facts and figures into the Creative Department of his mind for it to reshape and assemble and toss back to him in finished form.

Eventually, through the relaxed sleep state or twilight zone of consciousness, new inventive ideas were produced. Edison knew that his conscious mind possessed no creative power whatsoever—and that, when he had studied consciously long enough, he had to get himself out of the way and let Mr. Subby take over.

All creative geniuses are exercising this same creative power of mind. Many top executives follow the practice and keep a cot or couch in their inner offices. For a few minutes each morning and afternoon, they instruct the secretary to hold all calls, while they relax and take a cat nap from which they awaken refreshed and revitalized, and often with the solutions to former pressing problems.

But the most effective moments in "creative sleep techniques" are obtainable at home, after you retire for the night. Here, with the day's cares and activities over and your mind's attention withdrawn from all external demands, you are then free to give thought to *your* individual needs.

What has been troubling you during the day? What hasn't worked out as planned? Has some happening disturbed you emotionally? Have there been any personality conflicts with any of your associates in business or members of your family? Have economic problems arisen which seem beyond solving? Is your health everything you think it should be?

Once the day's work is over, many of these concerns will surface if you do not try to suppress them. It would be helpful if you would form the nightly habit of taking a few minutes' inventory of your day. Try to see yourself as others may have seen you, ask yourself why things went wrong (if they did) and how could you have given a better account of yourself? What did you need to have done better? Picture how you can and will improve your attitude and actions in the future. You should awaken refreshed and revitalized, ready for the new day!

The dream state is one of the most mysterious and least understood aspects of consciousness. Many people mistakenly feel that "man knows not anything" when he is asleep. Actually, the subconscious part of man never sleeps—its activity continues after the conscious mind is at rest.

When you dream, *what* you dream is often brought about by bodily processes, by your fears and worries, by unfinished business which you haven't been able to let go, and by repressed desires which, once released from your conscious mind's control, are expressed in fantasy form.

These are surface areas of subconscious mind activity during sleep. They are usually disorganized and somewhat fragmentary in nature. But there are depths of the subconscious where the creative processes take over, and your extrasensory faculties begin to function, seeking to materialize in your outer life the images you have implanted of what you want to do or be or have.

This is the area of subconscious creative activity that you should learn to *utilize*, instead of depending upon its otherwise haphazard performance. Your subconscious must have direction at all times. If you pour into its vast creative reservoir all manner of thoughts and feelings about your day's operations, good and bad, it will give back to you unsettled and often garbled experiences in your future.

It must be emphasized again that your subconscious does not reason. Your reasoning faculty belongs to your conscious mind alone. If you fail to realize what you are doing to yourself through wrong thinking, your subconscious will not warn you! It will simply go to work to produce for you, faithfully and unquestioningly, whatever mental and emotional images you pass on to it. And while you sleep it will carry on its magnetic attraction, setting up conditions for you that you will encounter in a future moment of time—*unless* you change your picturizing!

When the Bible reports Job as saying, "What I feared has come upon me," he was recognizing that by his wrong visualization, he had helped create the very things he didn't want to have happen.

When you go to sleep nervous and upset about something, fearing the worst or feeling woefully inadequate about some situation, you can depend upon it: conditions are not likely to be better in the morning!

There is no way of escaping the consequences of your thoughts if you have taken your troubles to bed with you. They may have been momentarily removed from your conscious awareness, but they are still very much alive in your subconscious, which you have not programmed to help you by an injection of positive thought images designed to replace the negative.

You are creating your future each day by the nature of your thinking, and one of the best ways to better your condition in life is while you sleep! It only requires the investment of about fifteen minutes at bedtime. Many spend a few moments in prayer, asking their conception of God to help them, forgetting or not taking too seriously the age-old admonition, "God helps those who help themselves."

Never forget this: You were bestowed by your Creator with a creative power of mind, upon which you were intended to draw to produce for you the good things of life. This is the Higher Power within that functions for you when you pray, but it is not enough to ask for help. As a creature of free will and free choice, you are supposed to be *doing* what you can for yourself—and all you need is to *think* right to make most things turn *out* right.

The wife of a top executive wrote me recently to tell me that her husband had lost his position, had advertised and tried to get a new job in every way. But he was past the established employment age, and he had become terribly depressed and despondent, to the point of contemplating suicide.

"What can I do to give him new faith in himself?" she asked. "I've tried to interest him in positive-thinking books, but he says that stuff is all bunk. I am much concerned that if something good doesn't happen for him soon, he may be self-destructive."

In my reply, I state my conviction that a man of her husband's capabilities was bound to find acceptable employment if he began to picture himself as being able to adapt to a new kind of work, based on some hitherto-unrealized past experiences. But such an opportunity would never come to him unless he started visualizing it.

I enclosed a copy of a "Suggested Meditative and Visualizing Technique," which I had sent out to hundreds of correspondents. I told her if her husband would practice this thinking each night before retiring, I felt certain that he would find suitable employment within a three-month period. "But he has to mean every word of this meditation," I insisted, "or it will not work for him."

The Meditation

The way to live each day in the God Presence is to prepare for it in your meditation period the night before.

Give thanks for the protection and guidance you have received that day.

Picture what you wish to accomplish the following day...

Ask help from the God Power within—in support of your efforts to achieve—and to solve problems.

Put aside all fears and worries...

Do not let them reside in your consciousness overnight—or they will separate you from contact with the God Presence.

Then give yourself over to the care and protection of this Higher Power while you sleep.

When you awaken in the morning, give thanks for your life— your loved ones—and the new opportunities awaiting you in this new day.

Resolve to do all you can for others as you move about your day's activities, realizing that, in serving them, you are serving this God Presence which is serving you.

Look for good things to happen, and do not be disheartened by apparent setbacks.

Always remember that God's time is often not your time. He may say "Wait!" when you want to say "Go!"

But know that in God's good time, good things will come—if you hold to your faith and your willingness to help God, help you!

After several months passed, this letter came from the executive's wife:

Dear Mr. Sherman:

Just a short note to relate some good news. Jim has a job with the District Health Department, starting the 17th of this month as the New Emergency Medical Regional Coordinator. Right up his various lines of work in the past. He had applied for this the 3rd of July. It is now September. He had just about given up hope of it coming through for him. However! It is a stimulating challenge. He is as excited as can be.

You told me it would take two to three months of positive thinking and picturization. I started in the middle of the month of June. Obstacles were thrown in our path so often, I was beginning to weaken . . . and at that point, Jim picked up where I had left off.

How can we ever thank you enough?

The husband himself wrote me a letter of appreciation:

Dear Mr. Sherman:

Your feeling and concern for me is one of the most humbling experiences of my life.

When my wife gave me your meditation and begged me to give thought to it, I started visualizing the last thing at night and the first thing in the morning, seeing myself finding a job suited to my abilities.

I got over my feelings of defeat and despair, and as I repeated your meditation, applying it to myself, a feeling of peace and calm came over me—such a feeling as I had not had for some months.

And then, it happened—just as you predicted it would, if I did my part. I am forever grateful. I can see now what I have done to myself in the past through my wrong thinking and what I need to do to assure a happier, more successful future.

Haven't you sometimes said, "I don't have the answer now. Just let me sleep on it for a while." This just may have meant a catch phrase—you needed time to consider. But perhaps you found if you took a little while to mull things over, ideas would come and your problems were solved. It wasn't so much your sleeping on it as your dreaming on it.

Picture your need, then toss the ball to your subconscious. Let it throw back the answers in the form of strong hunches to take a certain course of action, contact some person you hadn't consciously thought of, make a definite "yes" or "no" decision based on feeling rather than seeming logic—all of which lead to right, conclusive results.

There is an old expression, "Dreaming true." When you assemble all the known facts on a problem with the conscious mind and have gone as far as you can go, and you still seem to be at a dead end, then is the time to "go to sleep on it," with the faith that your subconscious is ready and willing to carry on where you have left off and *image* for you the steps you should take to get over the hurdle.

To go to bed with a grievance or bitter feeling toward anyone (especially a husband or wife or close member of the family) is not only upsetting to the body chemistry but a mandate to the subconscious mind to build upon your ill feelings during the night and attract more unhappy experiences to you. It never pays to "go to bed mad." You should resolve now if you haven't before, not to let an argument exist overnight. Make it a rule to be the first to say, "I'm sorry" whether or not you are as much to blame as the other. Someone has to give in, to offer to make amends, or what starts out to be a molehill of ill feelings can become a mountain, worsening each night that's allowed to pass without a reconciliation.

Approaching sleep each evening with a free conscience and a happy anticipation of the morrow is bound to attract good things and good feelings all around.

You can prepare your subconscious mind to give you "dream answers" to specific needs by a specific form of meditation. You will want to use your own words to personalize what you desire, but these suggestions may be of help:

To get a solution to a problem
"Determine for me what I need to know and to do to enable me to solve the problem I am facing. . . ."

To get an answer to an economic need
"Lead me to the person, persons, or sources that can provide the required financial aid. . . ."

To overcome difficulties of a personal nature
"Let me be given the wisdom to reach an understanding with the other party or parties that will restore confidence and goodwill. . . ."

To get guidance in affairs of the heart
"Let me be given the knowledge of what to say and to do to win back the affection and confidence of my loved one. . . ."

Your subconscious functions like a computer in sensing your problems and needs, as voiced or felt by you. It reports back to your conscious mind, in the form of symbolic images whose meaning you will have to interpret. Or you may receive a realistic pictorial sequence showing you just how to proceed, or get a definite flash, an unmistakable feeling of just what to do.

The greater faith you are able to exercise in this God-given creative power, the greater guidance and protection it will give you. It is functioning for you now and always has been, whether or not you have realized it. But now that you *know* how to consciously control and direct it, you can expect more and more dependable answers in facing all life's experiences.

Chapter Fifteen: How to Use ESP in Making Business Decisions

"Sophisticated corporate leaders are turning more and more to intuitive decisions when all the facts are in and the final 'yes' or 'no' has to be given to the Board of Directors."

Al Pollard

In writing my part of this book, I have tried to bring into sharp focus my own personal experiences in using the higher powers of mind. Having been in the field of marketing and selling all my life, I know if I cannot "buy" the product or the idea myself, I can never sell it.

So, with this thought in mind, I bring you, with permission of the publisher, some highlights of the interview James Grayson Bolen published in *Psychic* (now *New Realities*) in December 1974. I have selected a few paragraphs that reflect my personal feelings which Jim picked up with great sensitivity himself as we talked all one day in my office.

PSYCHIC: *How long have you been interested in things psychic?*
POLLARD: Oh, about forty years. So you can see I'm pretty comfortable with the field. I don't get intimidated or defensive if someone raises his eyebrows when I talk about ESP particularly in relation to business.

What got you interested?
An incident that happened while I was on the Little Rock Junior College football squad, when we were up against a real tough team. I vividly recall experiencing a strong feeling—accompanied by seeing an image—of hitting a ball carrier so hard he fumbled the ball, which I recovered and went on to score six points for the team. It later happened exactly as I had felt and seen it. That really got me to thinking about psychic phenomena and later the positive thinking technique associated with it.

In 1937, while working for the *Arkansas Democrat*, I began writing a column called "Life Today" which I wrote for thirty-five years. I found myself constantly trying to give answers in helping people learn how to get a handle on their lives. Many unexplainable things kept cropping up—particularly psychic things—and I kept probing into what it was all about.

And what have you found?
Well, it's been natural for me to think and work in terms

of pictures. I started drawing as far back as I can remember; pictures always fascinated me, and I'd been studying color psychology and linear dynamics for some time. In fact, I nearly chose art as a profession. In psychic terms, I didn't realize at the time the dynamics of this picturizing process, but later realized just what it means and particularly what it could do.

It's a system of creative thinking we can work at every day, not permitting fears or worries or setbacks or disappointments to upset our pictures. These pictures become the blueprints our creative power of mind uses to magnetize and attract to us conditions, circumstances, opportunities, resources, and even the people to help materialize for us in real life what we have visualized—be it good or bad.

Now I've also found that every one of us has the capability of visualizing the projects we desire to become reality. It seems to me the energy of thought is transmitted into matter.

That seems pretty far out, especially in conducting a business, believing what you visualize will come to pass.

Well, I believe in it enough to conduct my own business by it, as well as make it a part of the executive training program I offer.

What other ESP elements do you include in your program?

I try to get into the minds of managers the concept of living ahead of the present time frame by projecting ahead of today to the next few weeks, or months, or years. We try to probe the future and bring back answers, realizing that in the realm of mind there is neither time nor distance. These psychic ideas go hand in hand: picturizing what you want to happen in concert with what will be happening around you.

This also works with problem solving. You first have to understand the problem, and I mean the *real* problem. Probing the depths of the situation through *the sixth sense* will often reveal the root cause. A technique for making this work is asking your Subconscious Mind the question: "I wonder what the problem is or will be?" According to Harold Sherman, the key word here is "wonder," which triggers a chain reaction to get your intuitive processes going. If you get feedback, make a detailed list of answers you're getting. But most businessmen haven't realized that the human mind properly handled is more informative and accurate than our so-called highly accurate machines.

Do you consider yourself psychic?

Not in the classic sense, as Harold Sherman is. I do think I have an ability—as I believe everyone has—that I can use in a psychic dimension. And I do know I constantly rely on intuitive feelings. Any time I get a strong hunch, I act on it. Although if I'm not careful, my conscious, logical mind will argue me out of it for one reason or another.

What do your colleagues think about your views and beliefs?

They have been conditioned to me for a long time. They know I'm always involved in thought-provoking things and are always interested in hearing about them. I think that fewer and fewer business leaders are pooh-poohing this field.

How do you go about instilling this in people in business?

I begin at the basic level of self-interest, the most powerful force among people. But the emphasis is relating to the self-interest of *others*, not yourself.

Intuitive feelings for others is the key. Once you sense needs and wants of an individual, the next step is to share your own strengths and interests to reinforce those needs and wants. This approach is basic. It relates to any one-on-one conversation or to any meeting, large or small.

I created these basic ideas as "The SI-System of Self-Interest Dynamics." In developing this system of concern for the other person, I have also evolved a *humanized* approach. The president or manager must first understand his own self-image and how it affects others—his peers, his employees, his friends, his family.

Once the manager sees himself clearly, he knows what he must do to have others see him as he *wants* them to see him. This takes emotional discipline plus determination to make personality adjustments. Most important is to get the manager to accept the process of *positive* mental imagery for himself.

Once he becomes convinced that he can picture events and how he would like them to occur, he begins to get a new respect for psychic working tools. As he begins attracting toward himself the positive things he wants to happen, he gets the basic message which Harold Sherman has projected for many years: namely, that in the realm of mind, like attracts like.

So by picturizing your positive image and living ahead of the time frame, you attract to yourself those elements that bring about the happening you desire. Likewise, if you program your mind with negative pictures, you attract negative elements.

Has your interest in the psychic field affected your concept of the universe and God?

Certainly. I now feel that there are broader aspects to all of this; I feel I have grown and expanded my feelings and thoughts. You can't convince me any longer that God has whiskers; I have no reason to hold an image like that.

I also feel that I no longer have to think of God or the universe in terms of being Presbyterian—which I happen to be—or a Christian or Buddhist, or whatever. I have begun thinking in terms of a one-on-one relationship with the universal omnipotent power.

How about your philosophy of life and man's role in all this?

I think that everyone who is given life on this earth by the great creative universal force has an obligation to improve the world he lives in, and leave it a little better to the ones coming along.

Twenty-five years ago, ESP and syphilis were two words seldom used in polite society. Thanks to businessmen speaking out about ESP in their lives and thanks to penicillin, both words are now acceptable.

Many years ago, a Rotary Club program chairman called me on the phone in desperation.

"Al," he blurted almost breathlessly, "I'm in a jam, and you've got to help me."

"What's the trouble?" I asked with mild curiosity.

"My speaker just called and said he was drunk and couldn't possibly make his speech. I know you are always making speeches and I'm calling on you to make one in about forty-five minutes!"

The time was about 11:30 A.M., which was 30 minutes before the expectant membership would assemble for their pan-fried steak and green beans to be followed by group singing and a fine talk.

"I'll tell you what, George. I'll make you a speech if I can pick my own topic without any questions asked."

"You got it, Al! Can I depend on you to be at the hotel by noon?"

"Sure," I said with an inward smile—because I was going to spring ESP on these businessmen for the first time in their lives.

Well, to make a long story short, there wasn't too much Rotary reaction while I was talking. I did notice two or three heads nod off toward the back of the room. When I finished talking, there was the usual polite applause. Seemed to me I had struck out with a flourish.

But now came the surprise. About seven or eight Rotarians drifted up to the head table to say they enjoyed the talk. At least, these fellows seemed to have heard me.

To my surprise, these businessmen began to recite strange experiences, one after another, and asked me if these were ESP happenings.

They were genuinely interested in ESP and how it worked. Believe it or not, I stayed after the talk and visited with these men for over a half hour!

That experience convinced me the time had come to take ESP out of the closet and spread it around the business community of America.

By the way, ole George was pleased. He told me so himself. He allowed that my speech was sure better than a talk by a drunk. I had to consider just what that encouragement could mean to my ESP talking career.

Amazing ESP Experiences in Business

The greatest businessman/psychic I ever had the pleasure of knowing was Ambrose Worrall, husband of Olga Worrall, the internationally famous psychic and healer.

Ambrose was a delightful Scotsman with a soft voice and a constant twinkle in his eye. He was also an electronics engineer who had a very responsible management position with the Martin-Marietta Company. One evening, after one of our ESP Research Associates Foundation's annual seminars, he told me the following story:

"I remember quite well," he began with his little chuckle. "I received a frantic call from the president to come to his office at once. I wondered what was wrong.

"When I got there, the president told me we were within two days of making delivery of twenty-seven bombers to the government. If we were late, the penalty clause would be invoked, and our company would stand to lose a great deal of money.

"It seemed that in the return of one tray of ball bearings to the stock room, the wrong-sized bearings came back. They were one ten-thousandth of an inch too small."

These bearings were for the aileron structure in the wings. But these wrong-sized ball bearings—which had been installed in one of the twenty-seven planes—would make the wing malfunction and thus cause that one plane to crash.

"Well," Ambrose continued, "to have taken each wing section apart to search for the wrong-sized ball bearings would have taken days. We had only two days."

"So what did you do?"

"The president told me to get on the problem right away, and he asked me what I intended to do. When I told him I was going home to take a nap and see what should be done, he almost went through the ceiling!"

"And did you do just that?"

"Yes, I went home and concentrated on the need to identify which plane had the faulty ball bearings. I dropped off to sleep and awoke at about 10:00 P.M. with a strong inner feeling as to what I should do. Without delay, I dressed and went to the flight line. I aroused one of the flight mechanics and asked him to get a light so we could walk down the flight line of twenty-seven bombers."

"Did the flight mechanics wonder what in the world you were doing?"

"Oh, yes," Ambrose replied simply. "He knew I did strange things from time to time that no one seemed to understand."

"So what happened?"

"It was quite interesting," he replied. "I felt it necessary to stand for about five minutes in front of each bomber to see what kind of a feeling I would get. Nothing happened until I reached the seventh plane. Then a definite sensation in my solar plexus area told me I had found the faulty wing. I told the flight mechanic to get a complete crew and check out the ball bearings in the left side of the wing. We did. And sure enough, we found the wrong-sized bearings."

Ambrose told that story with a quiet, matter-of-fact style, which was his way. He amazed me again in a later conversation when he told me that he had a difficult time in his college calculus class. He said quite simply:

"Every time the professor would invite me to explain solving the problem on the backboard, I was forced to admit that I could give him the answer—but I couldn't tell him *how* to get it."

ESP and the Decision Process

In making sound decisions, every successful manager knows he has to face facts. Computer facts are accepted as gospel. Executives seem to feel quite comfortable with a sheaf of computer printouts piled high on their desks.

And yet computers only tell what, not *why*—and that's where confusion sets in more often than not. What happened is fiscal history. *Why* it happened is where the decision-making takes place. Probably one of the most valuable assets a corporation can have is the ability to bring creative answers to problems that seem to defy solutions.

Unfortunately, there is no one-two-three way to solve tough problems in large corporate operations. The best way to avoid corporate disasters is to have sound creative thought going into the product system *before* problems loom large through lack of creative insight.

Our American automobile industry is a good case in point. I recall years ago when I heard the sales manager of Ford Motor Company introduce a new little car they were calling the Mustang. This was the first American small-car response to the German Volkswagen. Some insightful executive at Ford could see the writing on the wall: that times were changing, and the market itself was changing. So Ford reacted with imagination. After the Mustang came the Pinto. Today, Ford's imports from England are even smaller.

Several years earlier, I recall reading articles by American car manufacturers stating the small imports were not much of a threat, but when they got to be, something would be done to combat them in the marketplace.

The time is now. And the going is rough for the manufacturers who can't seem to catch the confidence of American consumers. Quality, style, operation are at stake. Sales of foreign cars have now risen to approximately 30 percent of the total U.S. market!

All of which is to say that decision-making is more involved than reading figures and coming up with what seems to be a logical answer. Too often the people equation is ignored, and high prices are paid by those who make decisions based on "things" instead of people.

Outer Mind vs. Inner Mind

I have read many accounts of corporations at the crossroads of their operation that had to make sweeping decisions costing millions of dollars. If they were right decisions, great. If they were wrong decisions, heads would have rolled—top heads.

The working of this process has been validated by many chief executives whose desk wears the sign: "The buck stops here!" For it is here that the highest level of sixth sense decision-making takes place.

At this level, there seems to be a pattern to decision-making. Usually, the president is carrying the ball at the Board of Directors' meetings. He calls forth his top experts to present facts involving the big decision to be made. These facts are supported by tons of computer printouts which make everyone feel secure—except the president. He knows there's more to the decision than reading computer printouts. Hopefully he is aware of the people factor involved, because that's the name of the game today—pleasing consumers who have many choices they can make in the marketplace.

Of course, most executives who use their higher powers of mind in decision-making are aware that so-called facts given them can have been gathered erroneously. Hence conclusions based on these facts do not hold water.

This is where the executive's sixth sense comes into play. Through penetrating insight, the big picture is seen without the confusion of lopsided facts. This common sense some call experience, and knowing what to look for. The net result is that the record reflects executives with the best track record for making sound decisions have this sixth sense insight. Some call it knowing without experiencing.

One of the best examples of an industry in which this higher power of mind works is in oil field exploration. Several years ago I spent hours visiting with my good friend Bill Keeler, who was at that time the chief executive officer of Phillips Petroleum Company in Bartlesville, Oklahoma.

Bill has probably had a broader involvement in the oil patch than any other one petroleum executive. He's done it all. But like so many of the pioneers in this industry, his first love is "wildcatting" for new oil fields.

He has great respect for geologists he has worked with through the years. "But you know," he said with a twinkle in his eye, "when I used to go into the field before we drilled it, I conferred with our geologists to get the complete feeling for the area they thought we'd find oil. Then I would walk the area.

"When I got a strong gut feeling here in the pit of my stomach, I would know I had found the exact spot where we should stick a bit in the ground. The fact that I had a pretty darned good record of being right was enough to convince our geologists to follow my gut feelings."

Who can say where and how Bill Keeler developed

such a keen intuitive feeling for decisions and people? It's interesting to note that Bill Keeler was the grandson of a Cherokee Indian woman. He makes the point that both his mother and grandmother had frequent psychic experiences.

Among many of the honors and responsibilities Bill has received nationally, his work as chairman of the Board of the National Association of Manufacturers convinced him of one thing about intuition. "I discovered in talking with many of the executives I worked with in this association that many of them were using intuition in their decision-making process. Some of my friends called them gamblers, but I noted from their track records that they were usually right."

When judging people, I noted that Bill is slow to make a verbal judgment. I have observed he has a way of telling stories to give him more time to get a more in-depth feeling of the person under evaluation.

As chief of the Cherokee Nation from 1949 until 1971, he has done more to help his people establish themselves as the businessmen they once were before the Trail of Tears march from Georgia to Oklahoma. Bill tells with great pride how advanced the Cherokee Nation was before the U.S. Government unsettled their entire lifestyle.

The Publishing Business Calls for Intuition

Writing, editing, production, marketing, and sales are the working ingredients of a publisher. And yet that imponderable—intuition—is an important guide to publishing books that sell.

One of the finest examples of this overall publishing philosophy is Eleanor Friede, a charming young lady who owes her rise to fame to the publishing of *Jona-*

than Livingston Seagull, an uplifting book that sold 10 million copies, even though at Macmillan it was known as "Friede's Folly."

Hearing her story from her own lips was a very exciting experience. It happened in April 1980, when Ingo Swann invited Harold Sherman and me to dinner in his fourth-floor art gallery in the Bowery in New York.

With keen anticipation we pushed the doorbell at his Bowery stoop. As we waited, two fuzzy-headed winos hit me for two bits for another jug. As they staggered away, a very attractive woman, turned out with tailored precision, came striding up the stairs beside us. Before we could introduce ourselves, Ingo popped open his front door and did the honors.

The young lady was Eleanor Friede. And so began a long and fascinating evening.

Ingo launched the evening with champagne, and as the champagne flowed, so did the conversation.

I had the comfortable opportunity of asking Eleanor the story behind the publishing of *Jonathan Livingston Seagull.* I reminded her that her story had been presented in *Psychic* (now *New Realities*) when James Grayson Bolen, the publisher, featured an interview with me regarding the subject of ESP in business. (His was the first national publication to give credence to this area of higher-mind application.)

"Yes," she replied with an intriguing smile. "I remember the article quite well. I have a few questions I would like to ask you."

"Fine," I replied, "but first let's hear how you took *Jonathan Livingston Seagull* from an idea to a soaring publishing success."

"It's a rather long story, but I'll give you the key points. First of all," she said, "Richard Bach was a pilot teaching flying. He was not doing particularly well, so in his spare time he wrote the story of *Jonathan Livingston*

Seagull. Since I fly my own plane, I guess it was inevitable that the manuscript would find its way to me.

"I read the manuscript and reread it. The more I thought about it, the more I was convinced it would give readers a lift. It was turned down by a number of publishers, but I was finally able to convince the editor in chief at Macmillan to publish it. The rest is history. It sold better than 10 million copies and is still being purchased around the world."

"What turned you on?" I asked quietly while taking another sip of Ingo's champagne.

"It was a beautiful story and I knew what its power was—an uplifting story appealing to a broad cross section of readers. You see, I cannot function at peak if the 'vibes' are not right, even if all the visible signs are."

To me, the important point in Eleanor Friede's story is the ability to live ahead of the time frame and determine how people will *feel* about a manuscript—before it is published.

This same ability is used by top executives around the country. They have the ability to sense what will happen before it happens. This is not merely anticipating the future. This is bringing an insight into play which helps illuminate how people will react at a given point in time to a given situation.

Chapter Sixteen: How Women Use Their Intuition More Than Men

"Because a woman is usually more aware of women and men to achieve her goals, she is quicker to tune in on the feelings of others and what they will do."

Al Pollard

I'm not going to be so bold as to say women have more ESP than men. But I will say that women *use* their ESP more than men

How many times have you heard women around you say: "I just have a feeling this isn't going to work!"

And more times than not, they are right.

Why is it that women use their ESP in everyday life more than men? Did the Good Lord give them more ESP talent? I don't think so.

If you consider the history of woman, she has played a subservient role to man in all parts of the world. Perhaps it all started when cavemen had more strength and could go out in the world and kill the main course for dinner. As you take this basic relationship down through history, you see the superior strength of men playing the dominant role in the family as provider and protector.

Women have had little choice until the last hundred years of history. Now times are changing. But even today, women realize that if they are going to attract a man who will hunt and fight for them, they must have a feeling for what it takes to catch and hold the male's attention and loyalty.

Little girls learn this technique about as soon as they are aware of people. I have a granddaughter who learned as soon as she could toddle that the way to get what she wanted was to crawl up in my lap in my big chair, roll those beautiful brown eyes at me, and say something like: "Granddaddy, you know how much I like those little red candies you bring me. . . . Well, could I have just one more piece before I have to go home?"

For some strange reason, many men feel uneasy about verbalizing what they really feel and want from a woman. For the men who have this difficulty, women are quick to *sense* nonverbal language and respond quickly. On the other hand, there are men who are quite suave at doing and saying what a woman would like to hear. This is his way of getting what he wants from a woman. Again, it's the lady's ESP to the rescue. If she doesn't want to be taken in by such a male type, she *senses* very quickly what is about to happen. In either instance, it's the sixth sense guiding her.

One of my favorite people-watching games is to sit and observe all the subtleties between two or three women talking among themselves. Unless they are the very closest of friends, there will always be a "game" being played one way or another. The fun is to watch the body language and listen to the words as they bounce and slide back and forth. I have observed that women with higher education sharpen the game considerably, zinging each other with great finesse and aplomb.

A Woman's Intuition in the Business World

In the area of business, can a woman square off against a man and trade blow for blow? Often "office power" is still on the side of the man. Smart women know this, but knowing it just changes the tactics of the game. So out comes the woman's intuitive power for winning without trading blows.

It has always been my observation that the busi nessman and his secretary who get along best are the ones that share mutual desires for survival in business. I have great respect for women's ability to survive anything. They seem better at it than most men. So when they line up with the boss they respect and use their ESP powers for the good of the two of them, you have a sound operation.

Let's take a specific situation and see how it works.

The boss is faced with the challenge of putting together a very important meeting. He is to conduct the

meeting and achieve certain areas of consensus to free up
promotion projects that need to be handled as quickly as
possible.

This boss is smart enough to have his secretary in
on his plans for the meeting from the very start. He has
always informed her of the inner workings of his business
so he can have a sounding board for his ideas. He knows
from experience that she has feelings about situations
that are important to a sound decision. So the first thing
he asks regarding the upcoming meeting is: "How do you
think Jim Arnold, the executive vice-president of Midwest
Beverages, will take to my idea of a joint promotion? His
company will probably be the largest contributor based
upon his volume of business."

The secretary is silent for a moment as if getting a
feeling on the question. Then she slowly replies: "I have a
hunch he isn't going to like it at first, for the reason you
just gave. It seems to me you need to sell the smaller distributors first. Once he sees that they are all willing to
pitch into a joint effort, he'll begin to see why it is to his
benefit to go along. If you ask me, selling the smaller distributors is the key to your total success."

Of course there was much more to this discussion.
But to make the point, let me tell you how the actual
meeting was handled to achieve the consensus the boss
was seeking.

The boss had done his intuitive homework. He had
given much consideration to the smaller distributors and
what they could gain from this proposed promotion. He
had tried to experience this meeting before it actually
occurred.

According to his game plan, he presented a promotion that would cover all the territories served by these
distributors. It was true that Jim Arnold, executive vice-

president of Midwest Beverages, had the largest territory of all. He also had the choice metro markets.

Based on his case sales per month, he was going to be paying about three times more than any other distributor. And he could be outvoted on any decision based on the "one company, one vote" operation of the group.

Knowing all of this, the boss followed his secretary's hunch. He began making point after point that would be helpful to the smaller distributors. Once or twice Jim Arnold broke in to ask an operational question or two, but the boss got right back on the track of selling the smaller distributors.

After much discussion pro and con on this promotion, it was Jim Arnold who brought it to a head:

"When I first heard this plan presented, all I could think of was how much it was going to cost me. But I managed to keep quiet. Now that we have talked it over, I see how the money we will be spending together can have a rub-off in my territory. But I've got to admit that it took all of you fellows to sell me on the idea. So I say let's do it—but let's do it right!"

The point is obvious: The key to the success of the meeting was pointed out by the secretary who had a hunch, an intuition, a feeling—an ESP experience on what would happen.

There's no doubt that her business experience played an important role in this feeling. But the fact remains that she gave an objective reaction to a specific question, and it turned out to be highly accurate.

A Woman's Intuition in the Home

Mothers are much closer to their children than men are.

There is case after case recorded where mothers have been awakened in the middle of the night with the horrible feeling that a son or daughter is in deep trouble —maybe dying or dead.

This sort of experience frequently happens during wartime when loved ones are out on the firing line. I recall one case where a sailor's mother had a terrible dream experiencing the actual drowning of her son on the high seas. She told how after this terrible dream, she awoke suddenly to see her son actually standing by her bed. He was dripping wet and had seaweed hanging from his clothes. According to her story, she received a message from him telling her not to worry, that he was all right even though he had lost his life when his ship was torpedoed. The next week she received the formal telegram that her son was missing in action on the high seas.

According to Harold Sherman's experience, mind-to-mind communication is strongest when the sender is under emotional stress. This probably accounts for the fact that so many mothers receive death messages from sons and daughters.

Yet another side to mothers' ESP talent in the home has to do with living ahead of the time frame. Frequently this type of experience involves a member of the family and comes to the mother in dream form. I am thinking of one case that came to our ESP Research Associates Foundation office that told of such a dream.

A mother had a dream that her daughter was going to be driving her car and was going over an embankment to be killed by the impact. Upon awaking the next morning she pleaded with her daughter not to take the trip she had planned that day in her car. The daughter could not be persuaded. At the end of the day, the mother received a call from the sheriff in another county giving her the bad news that her daughter had been killed when her car went over a high embankment on a sharp curve.

When to Listen to a Woman's Intuition

There is a difference between a woman's intuition and anxiety. I have observed that women are often victims of their own worries. Some are always telling you things like: "I'm so afraid for John. He shouldn't be playing football. I just know he's going to get hurt!" Sometimes they actually seem disappointed if John *doesn't* get hurt.

Then you often hear this: "You just shouldn't take this chance. If anything goes wrong, you run the risk of losing everything you own. Won't you change your mind?" Many women are too overly cautious because they have been burned one way or another in life.

It appears to me that many women are deeply concerned with their own security. This is understandable since many are forced to live by the whims of the man in their life. Naturally they have a feeling of insecurity, and "playing it safe" often gets to be a way of life.

But this very anxiety for security can often color a woman's decisions. In my own life, I have never asked a woman to help me make a decision that involved great risk-taking. Few women like to live on the edge of a cliff.

Yet when a man finds a woman who stands by him and faces life shoulder-to-shoulder, they make a great team. When a wife or secretary says: "You can do it! I know you can!," there is great inspiration to a man seeking his path to the top. Every step can be treacherous—or it can take you that much closer to your goal in life. And believe me, women can have a tremendous influence in helping you take that perilous step!

Epilogue:
How to Use ESP in Your Everyday Life

"There is no limit to the state of awareness you can acquire to give you daily guidance and protection."

Harold Sherman

To live each day under the guidance of your higher powers of mind should be the ideal objective in life.

Because of the stresses and strains of present-day living, the physical, mental, and emotional demands on the average person, such an assigment is not easy to maintain.

"I know better," many have said to me, "but I just can't seem to control my feelings at times, to keep certain fears and worries and frustrations and frictions with others from getting me down."

Of course, it is difficult! But the only way to improve your conditions in life depends upon the use you make of your mind.

I am often asked how a person can begin to develop his or her intuitive faculties or extrasensory powers of mind. People say to me: "I'd like to be able to believe in ESP, but so far as I know, it's never happened to me, and I don't think it ever will."

I point out to them that so long as you doubt the existence of this power, you will short-circuit it, and it will not function for you. It is necessary, at the start, to accept on faith that you *can* receive and recognize what you may call "hunches." And when these feelings come into consciousness, decide to follow them, as best you can, in order to prove them out.

It would be helpful to keep a little dated notebook and to record impressions that come to you and seem as though they may have some significance. Often, you will find that impulses to do or not to do something or to proceed in a certain manner will appear to be without reason. Your conscious mind may try to argue you out of following such impulses. But when you do, you are amazed to discover that reasoning alone would not have served you as well! A few such demonstrable experiences gives your faith in these higher powers a great boost. You soon learn how to tell the difference in feelings between imagination or wishful thinking and the functioning of your genuine extrasensory powers.

When you have formed the daily habit of relying upon your exercise of intuition to back up your ordinary functioning of the five physical senses, you will find yourself making decisions in big and little matters with much greater confidence and assurance. You will be operating as a whole person—manifesting on the three levels of body, mind, and spirit.

In this highly materialistic day and age, we have been depending largely upon body and mind and somehow, neglecting the spiritual side of our nature. Through a study and practice of ESP, many of us are discovering our "real selves" for perhaps the first time and as a consequence, are achieving much greater happiness and success.

It helps immensely if husband and wife or a mutual friend can share your interest in ESP and utilize its practice together. Having the occasional evidence of a telepathic exchange of thought; visualizing the same objectives, thus adding to the power of your own thinking; and using similar meditations for your minds to work on while you sleep aid greatly in self-development.

Unless you program your life to some degree, you cannot expect these inner mental faculties to operate with regularity. If you and your husband or wife (or an understanding and interested friend) decide to work as a team, you can set aside a short time to read some inspirational material, leading up to a brief meditative period during which you visualize what you need for your individual and collective benefits.

If you have private concerns you wish to correct through visual action, take some extra moments to plant images in your subconscious. It will use them as blueprints to magnetically attract the opportunities and conditions required to bring about desired changes in you and your personal life.

Setbacks and disappointments occur in every individual's life. At times, they often result in loss of faith in friends and acquaintances, even relatives. Under certain circumstances, it is difficult to avoid feelings of hate and resentment that cause you to carry images of these unhappy experiences in consciousness, to further damage the health of your body and mind. Once something has happened, you or others cannot undo it. But you can be prepared to let go of any wrong emotional reactions, removing images of any undesirable event so that they do not attract more of the same in your future.

It will help if you associate your thinking with your concept of God by recognizing the existence of a Higher Power within. You may or may not have thought of identifying your daily activities with the idea of a God Presence. If you follow these suggested meditative practices, however, you will find that they will give you an inner assurance and an ability to face problems in a more effective and decisive manner.

Here is a Formula for Everyday Living, which you can repeat each night before bed, to prepare yourself for a better day on the morrow. It will help clear your consciousness of any disturbed feelings you may have acquired during the day.

• Each night I review the day's activities. I try to see myself as others may have seen me.

• I picture how I might have improved on my thoughts and conduct. Then I replace bad pictures with good, so they will not remain in consciousness.

• Following this, using my imagination, I project myself ahead in time and picture what I desire to achieve in life.

• I see good things coming to me on the morrow. Then I give myself over in sleep to the care and protection of God, the Great Intelligence, in the faith that I will awaken in the morning—refreshed, revitalized in body, mind, and spirit—ready for the new day.

By maintaining this daily attitude of mind, you will keep the channel open for the functioning of your extrasensory or higher powers. As you establish the habit and expectation of receiving inner guidance, you will be able to recognize and act upon the "hunches" that come to you, thus adding new meaning and purpose in your life.